150 Best Interior Design Ideas

150 Best Interior Design Ideas

Francesc Zamora Mola

HARPER
DESIGN

An Imprint of HarperCollinsPublishers

150 BEST INTERIOR DESIGN IDEAS
Copyright © 2017 by LOFT Publications

HarperCollins books may be purchased for educational, business, or sales promotional use.
For information, please email Special Markets Department at SPsales@harpercollins.com.

First published in 2017 by:
Harper Design
An Imprint of HarperCollins*Publishers*
195 Broadway
New York, NY 10007
Tel.: (212) 207-7000
Fax: (855) 746-6023
harperdesign@harpercollins.com
www.hc.com

Distributed throughout the world by:
HarperCollins*Publishers*
195 Broadway
New York, NY 10007

Editorial coordinator: Claudia Martínez Alonso
Art director: Mireia Casanovas Soley
Editor and texts: Francesc Zamora Mola
Layout: Cristina Simó Perales

ISBN 978-0-06-256912-7

Library of Congress Control Number: 2016958632

Printed in China
First printing, 2017

CONTENTS

6   **Introduction**

8   Yellow House
20 Back Bay Town House
36 Chestnut Place
56 AA House
70 Auburn Villas
80 Sandringham Residence
92 Toy House
100 Brighton East Interior
110 Hawthorn Residence
124 Architectural Mews House
140 Redpath
156 Edge
170 Bletchley Loft
182 738 Broadway
190 Saint Martins Loft
202 House MM
212 Luna House
224 Greenwich Village Town House
230 Graham Road
246 The Maryland

254 Madison Avenue Duplex
268 Urban Vibrancy
274 Concrete Jungle
282 Yaletown Loft
290 A.D. House
298 Paris Apartment
308 310 E 53rd Street
322 Fifth Avenue Modern
330 La Jolla Beach Cottage
348 Modern Farmhouse Cottage
356 Loft Great Jones
370 Loft Lovell
384 Duplex Penthouse Apartment
398 East Coast
414 Interior Villa
426 Penthouse V
440 De Korendrager
452 Downtown Loft
462 Soho Loft
472 Loft Apartment

478 **Directory**

INTRODUCTION

In contrast with the traditional concept of the home, where rooms were clearly differentiated and fulfilled very specific functions, current interior design trends are paving the way toward a flexible and modular use of space that efficiently adapts to the needs, tastes, and lifestyles of its occupants, favoring comfort and convenience.

This volume offers decorating ideas and inspirational tips through examples of exquisite interiors, boasting a plethora of modern design solutions, including open and spacious living areas, functional kitchens and bathrooms of all sizes and styles, and comfortable bedrooms. All these interiors have been conceived to fulfill the requirements of contemporary living in a variety of contexts: from idyllic beach getaways and modern farmhouse cottages featuring comfortable furnishings and relaxed elegance; through industrial warehouses converted into spacious and airy dwellings with original heavy ceiling beams and brick walls; to urban town houses and apartments that make the most of urban living by opening up their interiors to airy terraces with skyline views.

Spaces are often stripped of partitions in benefit of open and airy interiors, creating visual links between adjoining rooms and organization axes; leaving columns as support for sliding panels and cabinets, which in turn serve as space organizers; creating spaces that can be used independently or continuously to adapt to different uses.

Probably the kitchen and the bathroom have experienced the most noticeable changes: the kitchen, as a renovated heart of the house, is, whenever possible, a place for social interaction, a meeting point for family reunions and the entertainment of groups of people.

The bathroom ceases to be an isolated room tucked into the back of a house. It becomes a room that evokes wellness. In some cases, it becomes part of the bedroom, in what we call "en suite."

The styles tend to combine eclectic elements that reflect the multiculturalism of our societies, incorporating exotic artifacts, patterned fabrics, and art pieces. Sometimes design concepts borrow from previous eras: when dealing with existing structures, designers often consider the history of the space they are dealing with, as a means to inspire a design approach. When it comes to finishes, we've never had so many material, color, and texture options. These are the tools designers use to create living spaces that are just as visually inviting as they are functional, and that are empowered with personality and emotion.

Yellow House

Diego Revollo

São Paulo, Brazil

© Alain Brugier

Yellow House is an elegant 4,845-square-foot home, remodeled to reflect the owners' taste for interior decoration. The project also fulfills the requirement for the creation of a home suitable for entertaining. While the new design maintains the room organization and respects the original character of the house, doors were eliminated, and openings were made larger to allow for abundant natural light in the interior and to promote a fluid connection between spaces. In terms of the decoration, Yellow House features a sophisticated mix of antiques and contemporary furnishings that creates a unique and timeless environment.

001

The organization of the house was maintained, but removing doors and enlarging openings allowed for the creation of visual links between rooms, improving the perception of space.

Floor plan

A. Garden
B. Garage
C. Entry porch
D. Entry hall
E. Lounge
F. Living room
G. Dining room

H. Family room
I. Home theater
J. Powder room
K. Pantry
L. Kitchen
M. Service courtyard
N. Veranda

O. Laundry room
P. Outdoor dining area
Q. Maid's room
R. Storage
S. Bathroom

002

The entry hall, vestibules, and staircase are illustrative of the house's classical formality, putting emphasis on basic elements of design, such as proportion, scale, and symmetry.

One space succeeds another through wide doorways, creating axes of furniture arrangements and extending sight lines toward windows and focal points.

Light colors predominate in the large social rooms of the house, promoting activity and interaction, while dark colors are used in small rooms, creating cozy and tranquil atmospheres suitable for relaxation.

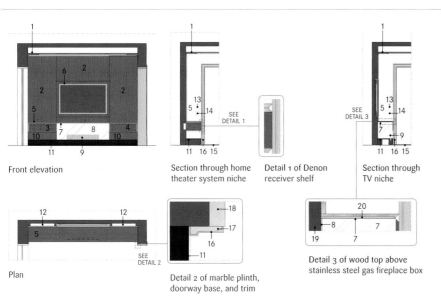

Front elevation

Section through home theater system niche

Detail 1 of Denon receiver shelf

Section through TV niche

1. Plaster molding
2. American oak paneling
3. Blu-ray player and HD-decoder shelf
4. Denon receiver shelf
5. American oak top
6. Niche clad in American oak
7. Stainless steel gas fireplace box
8. Back of the gas fireplace in tempered, mirrored glass
9. Extra clear 19 mm thick glass fixed to marble base
10. Back of niche in American oak
11. Emperador brown marble plinth
12. Cavity for wiring
13. Fireplace ignition switch
14. Switch
15. Wood flooring
16. Doorway base
17. Doorjamb trim
18. Doorjamb paneling
19. Existing masonry
20. Rockwool insulation

Plan

Detail 2 of marble plinth, doorway base, and trim

Detail 3 of wood top above stainless steel gas fireplace box

Entertainment center at home theater

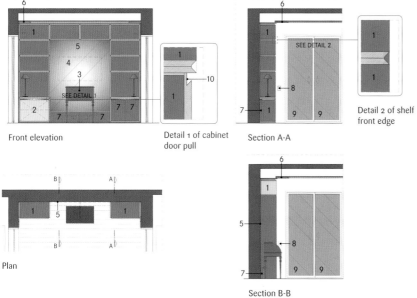

Front elevation

Detail 1 of cabinet door pull

Section A-A

Detail 2 of shelf front edge

1. Lacquered bookshelf, satin finish
2. Lacquered cabinet front, satin finish
3. Existing console table
4. Existing artwork
5. Beveled mirror
6. Plaster molding
7. False back with push-release latch to access wiring
8. Switch
9. Sliding door
10. Stainless steel plate

Plan

Section B-B

Bookshelf at home theater

003

The family room is on axis with the dining room—and with the kitchen. The two rooms have built-in cabinetry along the windows that provide convenient storage for tableware.

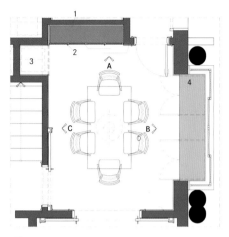

Plan

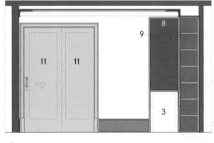

Elevation B

Elevation C

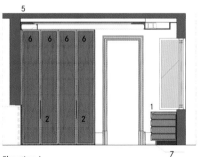

Elevation A

Family room

1. Lacquered cabinet
2. Stainless steel pull
3. Wine storage
4. Nanoglass top
5. Plaster molding
6. 5 mm recess
7. Stainless steel cabinet base
8. Lacquered paneling with 5 mm recess
9. Decorative plates
10. Shelf in American oak, natural finish
11. Sliding door, lacquered finish with 5 mm recess
12. Cabinet front, lacquered finish, push-release latch

004

Symmetry, balance, and visual
axes can enhance the formal
character of a dining room.

005

Patterns can be used to draw the eye to specific points and create dramatic visual effects. For instance, the tile used in the floor of the kitchen seems to continue up the wall behind the base cabinets and cooking range, all the way up to the ceiling.

Back Bay Town House

Boston, Massachusetts,
United States

© Michael J. Lee

This town house built in the late 1800s was converted into an apartment building in the 1960s. Later the building was once again remodeled to accommodate the needs of the new owners with three children. The remodel includes an additional set-back floor for a family room. The design approach has a contemporary sensibility and at the same time expresses great respect for the Boston town house typology.

The reconfiguration of an existing building can result in a series of interesting spaces, retaining the spirit of the original architecture and at the same time creating a contemporary feel.

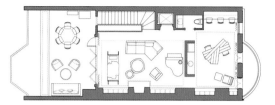

Fifth floor plan

Fourth floor plan

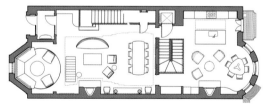

Third floor plan

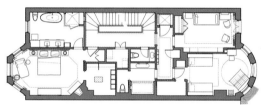

Second floor plan

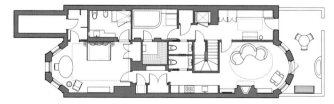

Ground floor plan

Metalwork is a recurring leitmotif throughout the house. Whether prominent features like staircase railings or striking details like fireplace screens, the variety of metal elements found in this home adds a unique touch to the décor.

007

Hallways and stairs are not just circulation areas. They are spaces able to hold their own with unique character and function.

The multicolor carpet on the stairs draws one into the house. The different colors used in the carpet harmonize with the colors used in various sections and rooms of the house.

UP TO FOURTH FLOOR

THIRD TO FOURTH FLOOR AND FOURTH FLOOR HALLWAY

FAMILY ROOM

UP TO THIRD FLOOR

STAIR HALL 303

SECOND TO THIRD FLOOR AND THIRD FLOOR HALLWAY

CORAL BEDROOM

HACIENDA BEDROOM

UP TO SECOND FLOOR

STAIR HALL 203

FIRST TO SECOND FLOOR AND SECOND FLOOR HALLWAY

MASTER BEDROOM

CHILDREN'S SUITE

COLOR KEY DMI #:	B1	B2	B3	C1	C2
TEXTSTYLE COLOR #: TEXTSTYLE STYLE #:	P8 – DB905	P6 – PL916 DCS#306(E)-3E	Q8 – BD906 DCS#306(E)-3I	A19 – BN902 DCS#306(E)-1	AN9 – BN907 DCS#306(E)-1

DMI #:	O1	O2	GN1	GN2	G1	G2
TEXTSTYLE COLOR #: TEXTSTYLE STYLE #:	C1 – PC901 DCS#306(E)-1	F1 – PC904	W9 – DG945	Y8 – DG9361	O9 – DB915 DCS#306(E)-1	N/A

Carpet color diagram

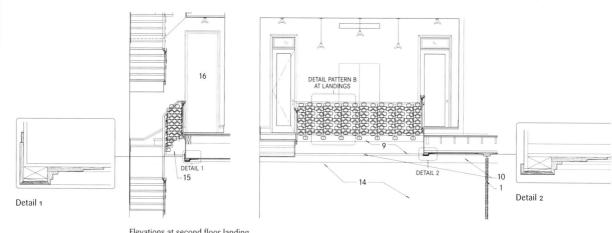

Detail 1

Detail 2

Elevations at second floor landing

16

DETAIL 1
15

DETAIL PATTERN B
AT LANDINGS

9

DETAIL 2

14

10
1

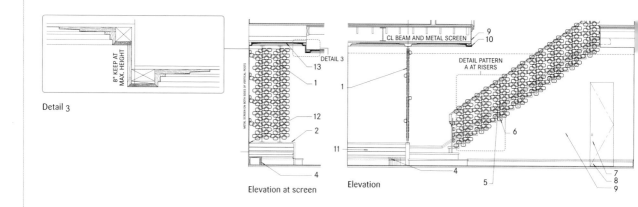

Detail 3

8" KEEP AT
MAX. HEIGHT

Elevation at screen

DETAIL 3
13
1

12
2

4

Elevation

CL BEAM AND METAL SCREEN

9
10

DETAIL PATTERN
A AT RISERS

1

11

6

4

5

7
8
9

METAL SCREEN ON BOTH SIDES OF VERTICAL POSTS

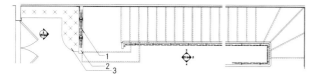

Partial plan

Staircase details

1
2
3

1. Custom metal screen, secured on top and bottom
2. Wood knee wall, painted
3. Platform bench with tufted cushion
4. Bench platform with applied baseboard, painted
5. Open metal railing attached to vertical posts
6. Solid mounting plate
7. Flush pivot door, painted

8. Wood base, painted
9. Gypboard wall, painted
10. Wood trim, painted
11. 4" wide strips, MDF, painted
12. Wood cap, painted
13. Raise ceiling trays at entry as high as possible
14. Open to living room
15. Gypboard side and underside, painted
16. Open to children's zone hall

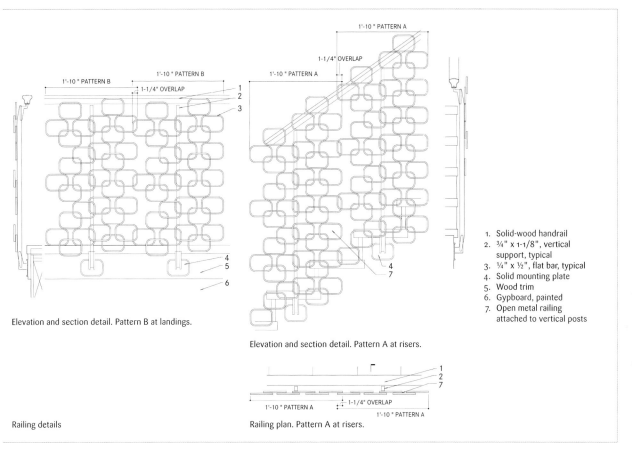

1'-10 " PATTERN A

1-1/4" OVERLAP

1'-10 " PATTERN B

1'-10 " PATTERN B

1-1/4" OVERLAP

1'-10 " PATTERN A

1
2
3

4
5
6

Elevation and section detail. Pattern B at landings.

4
7

1. Solid-wood handrail
2. ¾" x 1-1/8", vertical support, typical
3. ¼" x ½", flat bar, typical
4. Solid mounting plate
5. Wood trim
6. Gypboard, painted
7. Open metal railing attached to vertical posts

Elevation and section detail. Pattern A at risers.

1
2
7

1'-10 " PATTERN A

1-1/4" OVERLAP

1'-10 " PATTERN A

Railing details

Railing plan. Pattern A at risers.

008

Custom metalwork, as elements of separation between spaces, allow for light to pass through, while adding visual texture.

The kitchen shares the space with the breakfast area. The kitchen's back wall, island, and office desk with shelves are made of the same wood, unifying the space.

On the occasion of a remodel, walls are opened and doorways and various other openings are filled in to reorganize the space. Wall irregularities and former openings offer opportunities for the creation of cabinetry, making seamless design solutions.

Interior elevations at powder room on second floor

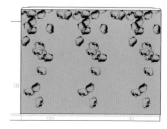

Elevation Natalie's wall

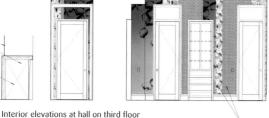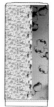

1
2

3

Interior elevations at hall on third floor

1. Bookcase mounted
   flush to wall
2. Continuous base trim
3. Plinth block, painted
   to match base trim
4. Wallpaper collage to
   be installed as noted

5. Continuous base trim
   behind plant block
6. Bookcase "Tree"
   provided by owner
   and installed over the
   wallpaper

4

5
3
6

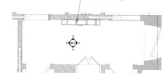

Plan of hall on third floor

010

Decorative wallpaper can help define areas and add visual interest, providing different spaces with their own identity. Wallpaper can offer an abundance of creative finishes, such as rich patterns, photographic images, and relief surfaces.

011

The use of wallpaper is not limited to covering all the walls of a room. Use decorative wallpaper to create wainscots and feature walls, which can act as accents that complement the color scheme of a space.

012

Just like wallpaper, tile can work wonders with visual and tactile textures, bringing an interesting look and feel to a room.

The family room on the top floor breathes a relaxed atmosphere, achieved through a palette of neutral colors and the soft shapes of the furniture. A suspended daybed brings in a playful touch.

Chestnut Place

BUTZ + KLUG architecture

Brookline, Massachusetts,
United States

© Eric Roth

The house, a significant part of Brookline's nineteenth-century residential history, had suffered through decades of piecemeal renovations, deferred maintenance, structural compromise, and ultimately foundation collapse. This condition presented the opportunity to reorganize the original, somewhat conventional central hall and circulation to take advantage of the unique site. The expanded and more porous living areas of the house are reoriented toward the rear garden with new south-facing loggia that wraps around the kitchen and connects the house to an adjacent indoor pool building.

The spacious living room nods to the historic roots of the house while providing framed views to the outside in all directions. The exterior deck can be accessed through either a set of new french doors or by walking through the flanking triple-hung windows when fully opened.

The wall of cabinetry continues from the kitchen into the media room as open bookshelves, creating continuity while also differentiating the spaces. The two sets of double doors, integrated with the cabinetry, can be used to close off the dining room from the media room.

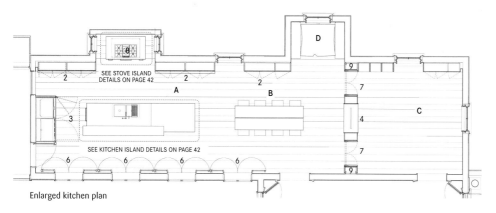

Enlarged kitchen plan

SEE STOVE ISLAND DETAILS ON PAGE 42

SEE KITCHEN ISLAND DETAILS ON PAGE 42

A. Kitchen
B. Dining area
C. Media room
D. Breakfast niche

1. Linear AC outlets integrated into top of cabinets and recessed to eliminate visibility.
2. Acid etched glass doors to conceal clutter yet add depth to the space.
3. "Technical unit" perforated metal cladding provides texture to the space and ventilation for concealed appliances.
4. View-through ethanol fireplace.
5. LED strip lighting integrated at each bookshelf.
6. 180 degree swinging french doors.
7. Integrated pivot doors to close off media room.
8. Custom stainless range island and vent hood above.
9. Vertical return air slots.

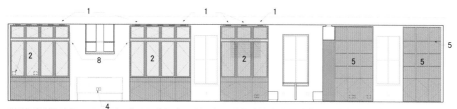

North elevation

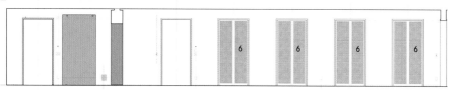

South elevation

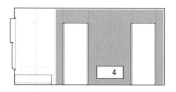

East elevation

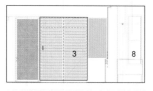

West elevation

013

The long proportions of the kitchen and dining area are oriented to reflect the loggia. This provides extended views and access to and from the exterior, creating a free flowing social space, while making the kitchen the new center of the house.

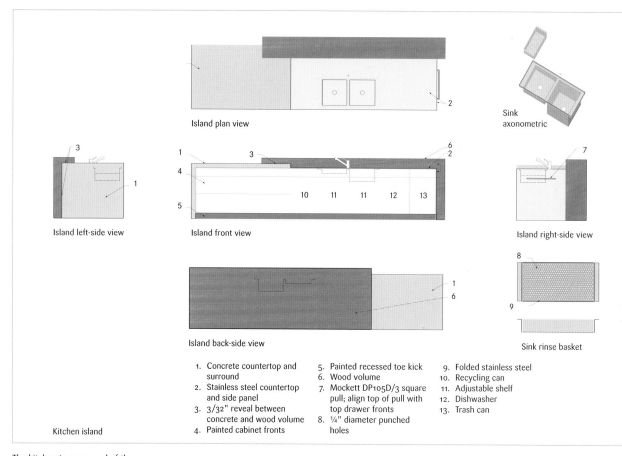

Island plan view

Sink axonometric

Island left-side view

Island front view

Island right-side view

Island back-side view

Sink rinse basket

Kitchen island

1. Concrete countertop and surround
2. Stainless steel countertop and side panel
3. 3/32" reveal between concrete and wood volume
4. Painted cabinet fronts
5. Painted recessed toe kick
6. Wood volume
7. Mockett DP105D/3 square pull; align top of pull with top drawer fronts
8. ¼" diameter punched holes
9. Folded stainless steel
10. Recycling can
11. Adjustable shelf
12. Dishwasher
13. Trash can

The kitchen is composed of three furniture-like elements: a central food preparation island with a sink, a cooking island flanked by floor-to-ceiling storage cabinets and a third "technical unit" cabinet at one end of the room that contains the refrigerator, freezer and combination ovens.

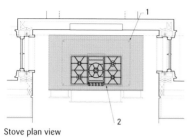

Stove plan view

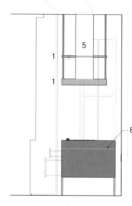

Stove front view

Stove side view

Stove island

1. 7/8" R fillet at the corners; align corners of radii
2. 36-inch **Gaggenau** cooktop integrated into stainless steel top; Remove stainless steel pan included with cooktop
3. 1-1/4" stainless steel shelf
4. Stainless steel shelf incorporating manufacturer's hood filter and lights
5. Painted plaster around hood exhaust duct
6. ¾" stainless steel tube (one at each corner)
7. Pull-out storage (6 total)
8. Reveal to match joint at front

This cooking island integrates a **Gaggenau** cooktop with a custom designed, freestanding, stainless steel base cabinet and drawers. Matching custom hood hangs above.

The loggia not only creates a wonderful place to have dinner, but it also shields the kitchen from the sun in the summer, while allowing it to extend indoors in the winter.

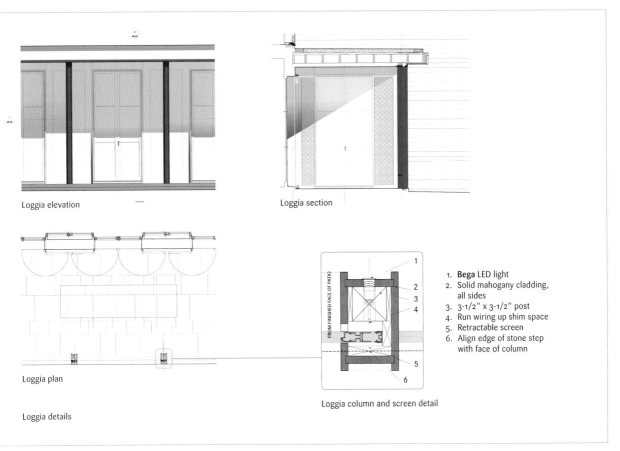

Loggia elevation

Loggia section

Loggia plan

Loggia details

FROM FINISHED FACE OF PATIO

Loggia column and screen detail

1. **Bega** LED light
2. Solid mahogany cladding, all sides
3. 3-1/2" x 3-1/2" post
4. Run wiring up shim space
5. Retractable screen
6. Align edge of stone step with face of column

014

The columns of the loggia contain retractable screens, allowing the building's interior/exterior threshold to expand or contract depending on the season.

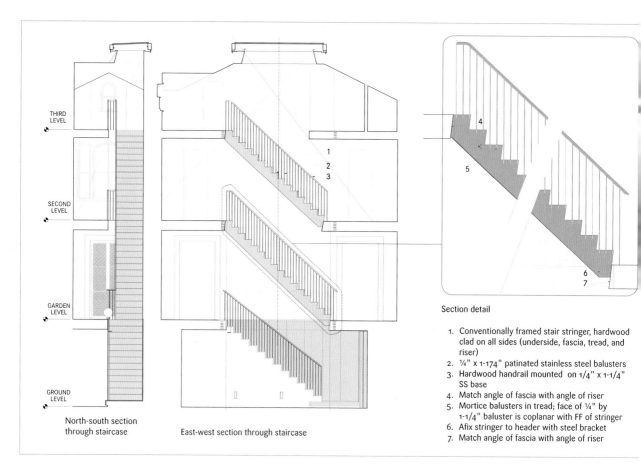

THIRD
LEVEL

SECOND
LEVEL

GARDEN
LEVEL

GROUND
LEVEL

1
2
3

4

5

6
7

North-south section
through staircase

East-west section through staircase

Section detail

1. Conventionally framed stair stringer, hardwood
   clad on all sides (underside, fascia, tread, and
   riser)
2. ¼" x 1-1⁄4" patinated stainless steel balusters
3. Hardwood handrail mounted on 1⁄4" x 1-1⁄4"
   SS base
4. Match angle of fascia with angle of riser
5. Mortice balusters in tread; face of ¼" by
   1-1⁄4" baluster is coplanar with FF of stringer
6. Afix stringer to header with steel bracket
7. Match angle of fascia with angle of riser

A new interior staircase opens up the
interior to a new level of clarity both
in terms of light and organization,
and terminates at the top floor in a
retractable skylight visible from the
entry level three stories below.

015

The fully operable skylight at the top of the stairs naturally ventilates the entire house when it is open (through stack effect), minimizing the use of air-conditioning.

Axonometric view of staircase

016

The large ornate mirror over an equally ornate console table echoes the shape of the rectangular window, balancing the two narrow, vertical windows. Together they create rhythm: window, mirror, window, framed picture, window.

017

The wall behind the bed was thickened to accommodate multiple chimney flues, but the corners became great niches for these custom steel shelf inserts.

A long mirror spanning the length of the vanity echoes the shape of the skylight above. It reflects the light filtering through the skylight and through the windows opposite the vanity.

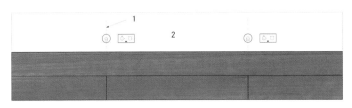

Bathroom cabinet front elevation

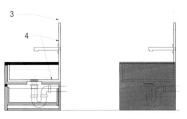

Bathroom cabinet
section

Bathroom cabinet
side elevation

Bathroom cabinet plan

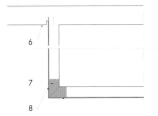

Bathroom cabinet plan corner detail

Master bathroom cabinetry details

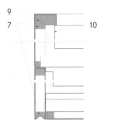

Bathroom cabinet section
through drawer face

1. Align CL spout with CL sink
2. **Corian** backsplash
3. Plane of wall
4. **Corian** sink and backsplash
5. **Corian** surface and sinks
6. Face of wall
7. Solid hardwood at corners
8. Hardwood veneer, grain
    continuous around each corner
9. Meiter **Corian** and hardwood
    with spline
10. **Corian** inside drawer lining

018

The teak vanity was designed
to accommodate the narrow
bathroom space. The wall
becomes the back of the sink
and the front edge is minimized.
The vertical dimension is also
minimized to enhance the sense
that it is a delicate piece of
floating furniture.

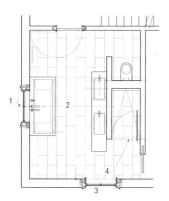

Enlarged bathroom plan

Bathroom north elevation

Bathroom WC west elevation

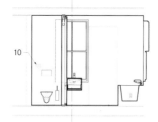

Bathroom south elevation

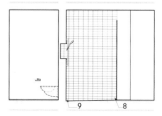

Bathroom WC east elevation

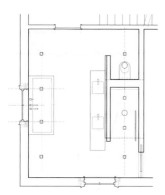

Bathroom RCP

Kids bathroom

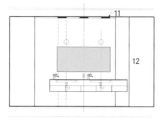

Bathroom east elevation

Bathroom west elevation

1. Start tile at center tub
2. Align tub and lavatory assembly with window
3. Center tile layout in width of room
4. No warmboard in shower
5. Flush temperature sensor, painted over
6. Locate handheld at center of wall
7. Align horizontal joints with side walls
8. Start full-width tile
9. Start full-height tile
10. Switches located on exterior wall beyond
11. AC outlets
12. Open to bedroom

019

The narrow vanity with side mounted faucets makes for a "kid friendly" bathroom. The extension of the vanity toward the shower provides needed space for towels and clothes. The green is both playful and a reference to the green roof on the loggia just outside.

Behind the apparent simplicity of the house's architecture is a complex interplay of volumes and planes that served as a reference for the new interior design. The goal was to achieve a cohesive whole. The interior of the house boasts horizontal and vertical planes, solids and voids, creating a succession of spaces, some of which are directly connected, others just revealed through screens of vertical fins.

AA House

Pascali Semerdjian Architects

São Paulo, Brazil

© Ricardo Bassetti

020

Symmetry contributes to the creation of well-balanced spaces. It can be achieved through the arrangement of furniture and the use of color and pattern, for instance.

The décor is made of both purchased and bespoke items, such as the entertainment center and other wood furnishings distributed throughout the house.

Watercolor view of living room

Second floor plan

Ground floor plan

A. Garage
B. Entrance
C. Entry hall
D. Storage
E. Bathroom
F. Cellar
G. Pantry
H. Back kitchen
I. Laundry room

J. Garden
K. Pool
L. Terrace
M. TV room
N. Kitchen
O. Dining room
P. Living room
Q. Bedroom
R. Closet

S. Maid's bedroom
T. Master bedroom
U. Master bathroom
V. Walk-in closet

The pieces of contemporary art were purchased in shops, galleries, and from private collections to specially fit into the design of the house interior. The artwork mainly features geometric shapes and blocks of color in a clear reference to the original style of the house.

021

The selection and the
arrangement of furnishings
in a room contribute to the
creation of a specific kind
of décor. For instance, clean
lines mix with organic shapes
to create a well-balanced
furniture variety, while accents
fall on color and texture.

022

As the quality of sliding-glass-door design and manufacturing reaches astonishing results—from an aesthetic and functional standpoint—glass door fittings are increasingly accentuated.

The brise-soleils on the exterior of the building served as inspiration for the creation of an interior layout based on a series of screens in various materials. These screens organize and separate the different spaces, while allowing some visual connection, making the space feel open and airy.

023

Create a dynamic and stimulating environment by mixing a variety of colors, textures, forms, and sizes. Then group them according to some of these categories to avoid a chaotic arrangement.

Heavily figured wood and colorful
lacquer finish come together in beautiful
nightstands, bringing into the room a
modern and playful touch.

Boys bedroom

Girls bedroom

Watercolor of different color schemes for nightstands

The design of the guest-bathroom sink required the making of a scale model to help the manufacturer understand its faceted form.

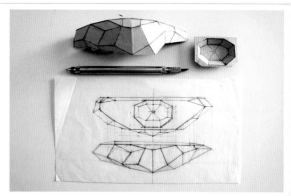

Guest-bathroom-sink model

024

The blocks of solid color—like the black finish of the soaking tub and the wood vanity— add a touch of color to this bathroom, where Carrara marble predominates.

Auburn Villas

LyonsKelly
Dublin, Ireland
© Mark Scott

The home was built in the 1980s with a restrictive layout and pokey rooms. Still, the owner purchased it because of its secluded garden and central location. Opening the house to the garden and creating a more dynamic entertaining space were the main design priorities. The scope of work also included the creation of a separate study off the main room and the makeover of the bedrooms and bathrooms. The decoration is a mix of Scandinavian restraint and more glamorous elements, such as the kitchen inspired by the design of a French bar.

The design firm devised a large barrel-vaulted living, dining, and kitchen area. These three functions are organized around a mid-height brick stove surround, yet the area has an open and airy atmosphere.

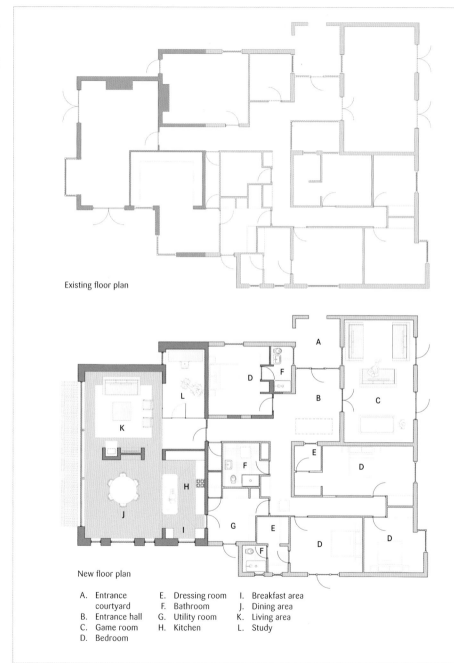

Existing floor plan

New floor plan

A. Entrance courtyard
B. Entrance hall
C. Game room
D. Bedroom
E. Dressing room
F. Bathroom
G. Utility room
H. Kitchen
I. Breakfast area
J. Dining area
K. Living area
L. Study

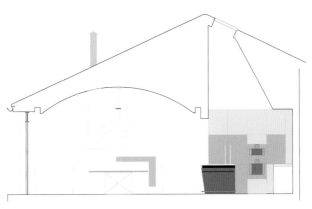

Section through dining and breakfast areas

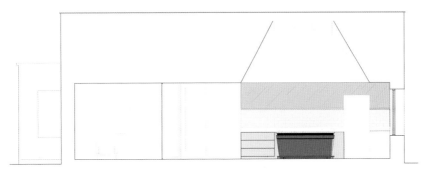

Section through living and dining areas

The vaulted ceiling over the living and dining area and the deep light well above the kitchen are unexpected forms under the traditional gable roof.

The vaulted ceiling made of wood slats defines the living and dining area and provides it with directionality.

The red kitchen island is a focal point, likely to attract a group of people around it, becoming the center of the living area.

025

The light tones of the
finishes in a room can be
complemented by textured
furniture to create a cozy and
warm atmosphere.

The study, off the main living area, offers a quiet reading and working space. The glass enclosure allows natural light from the bright living area, making up for the lack of windows.

026

Glass interior doors and skylights can be used to bring light into the middle of a house, provided that the house is a single-story building.

027

The design of this bathroom relies on pattern rather than on color to create a design statement. The floor tiles against the brick-bond-pattern tile work on the walls offer a clean yet visually striking look.

Sandringham Residence

Doherty Design Studio

Sandringham, Victoria,
Australia

© Derek Swalwell

Doherty Design Studio collaborated with Technē Architects
on a double-fronted weatherboard cottage. The bold form of
the new two-story extension allowed Doherty Design Studio
to create a fun, energetic home that provides for the needs
of a young family of four. The interior is a series of uniquely
personalized rooms with a simple, utilitarian aesthetic that
plays with materiality, bold graphic shapes in robust finishes,
and blocks of vibrant colors. Clean lines and simple but
functional detailing ensures a continuous artful connection
between old and new.

Second floor plan

A. Entry
B. Bedroom
C. Master
   bedroom
D. Dressing area
E. En suite
   bathroom
F. Bathroom
G. Laundry
   room
H. Study
I. Dining area
J. Kitchen
K. Pantry
L. Living area
M. Patio

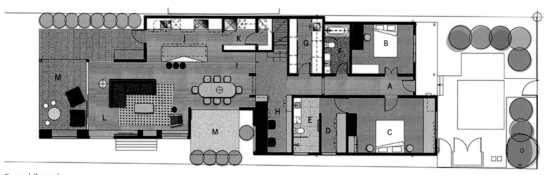

Ground floor plan

Irregular-sized boxlike timber steps and red staircase along a paint-drip feature wall meet the design brief for fun and color. A gridded wall is another strong element, which features circular cutouts as a display solution for wine bottles, adding a playful detail to the house design.

Fireplace, wood storage box,
entertainment center, and windows
are not conceived as separate elements.
They form a modular composition that
references the architectural design of
the extension.

028

The modular design of the fireplace wall is carried on to the kitchen. Play with scale, form, texture, and color adds to the graphic aesthetic, while pale wood-grain cabinetry and stools soften the look.

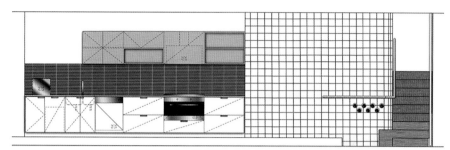

Kitchen elevation

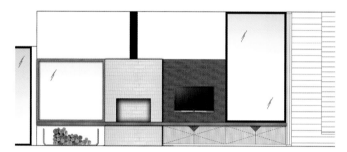

Living area elevation

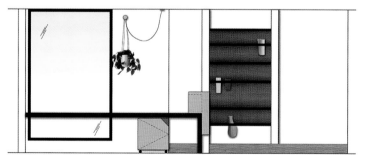

Study elevation

A perforated black folded screen is a key feature. It acts as a separation between old and new, while allowing visual connection. Additional color is through decorative items hanging from the screen and pendant lights above the dining table.

029

Maximize storage space with low cabinets below a window sill. In addition to increasing the storage capacity of a room, these low cabinets can double as benches.

030

Consider ceiling- or wall-mounted light fixtures near the headboard as an alternative to the traditional bedside table lamp. By doing so, you keep the bedside table clear for other items.

031

Unusual mirrors in the
bathroom can add visual
interest to a nondescript
décor. They can introduce
color and texture to support
other elements in the room,
which may otherwise stand
out awkwardly.

032

The use of a monochromatic color scheme in a bathroom challenges one to think about ways to give this room of the house a unique character. Play with shape and texture to add pattern in an understated yet powerful fashion.

Toy House

Pascali Semerdjian Architects
São Paulo, Brazil
© Ricardo Bassetti

This 2,660-square-foot home, located a few yards away from the client's main residence, was conceived as a large playhouse for a growing family. In addition to housing the children's toys, the building serves as a venue to host parties and events for all family members.

From the street, the discreet entrance opens up to a minimalistic interior that emphasizes the playful character of the colorful furniture and the display of contemporary wall art, sculptures, and the numerous games and toys.

The lower floor accommodates an open living area and a utility core, while the upper floor is a metal structure over a concrete deck that allows flexible configurations.

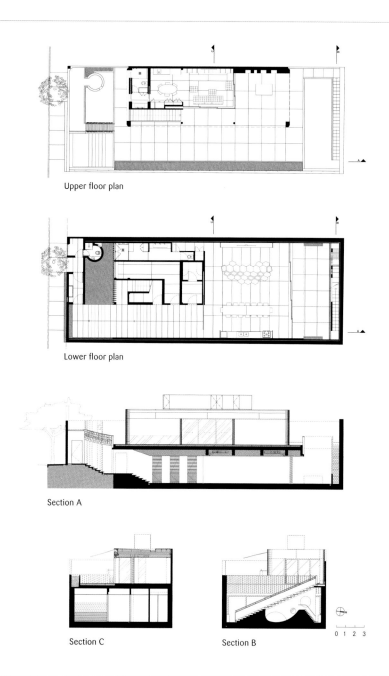

Upper floor plan

Lower floor plan

Section A

Section C

Section B

0 1 2 3

033

The use of sliding doors fits in with the principles of contemporary architecture, contributing to the aesthetic appeal of a construction. They also allow for maximum natural lighting and promote the connection between interior and exterior spaces.

A large collection of artwork is playfully integrated into the project. The various styles include graffiti by Brazilian artists Os Gêmeos, bold drawings by Keith Haring, and three-dimensional wall art by Anish Kapoor.

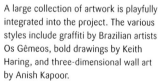

034

Modern technology has permitted the creation of sliding glass doors that can be as unobstructive as possible by means of minimal floor and ceiling rails.

035

Large awnings and shutters can
be used along the perimeter
of a structure to transform the
perception of an interior space
according to different needs.

The space on the upper floor can adapt to different activities, creating an indoor area that can be used all year round and can expand to the deck along two of its sides. Because of the way it was designed and constructed, it can be easily dismantled.

Brighton East Interior

Dan Gayfer Design

Brighton East, Victoria,
Australia

© Dean Bradley

Preferring to not build up, the clients wanted to ensure the
home they were returning to met the hectic requirements of
the family. The project encompasses a kitchen, bathroom, en
suite, and laundry room, as well as cabinetry throughout the
Californian-style bungalow. The bathroom and en suite interiors
are discreet, but the spotted gum cabinetry is both a focal
point and a link to materials employed in other rooms. Western
red-cedar lining boards, spotted-gum battens, and Russian-
birch plywood combine with steel, ceramic tile, and burnished
concrete, resulting in a flexible kitchen that adapts to the needs
of a young and energetic family.

A built-in plywood bookcase is one of the many custom-made pieces of cabinetry designed to rejuvenate the existing dwelling.

The floor plan is clearly defined by a central area that includes a living-dining area and a kitchen. The private zones are concentrated in three separate wings of different sizes, branching off the central area.

Floor plan

A. Entry
B. Bedroom
C. Bathroom
D. Family room
E. Living area
F. Dining area
G. Kitchen
H. Pantry
I. Laundry room
J. Breakfast nook
K. Study
L. Master bathroom
M. Walk-in closet
N. Master bedroom

The kitchen design combines the cool tones of the polished concrete, stainless steel, gray tile, white walls, and low cabinet laminate fronts with the warm tones of the two types of wood used on the island, the pantry and refrigerator wall, and the cabinets.

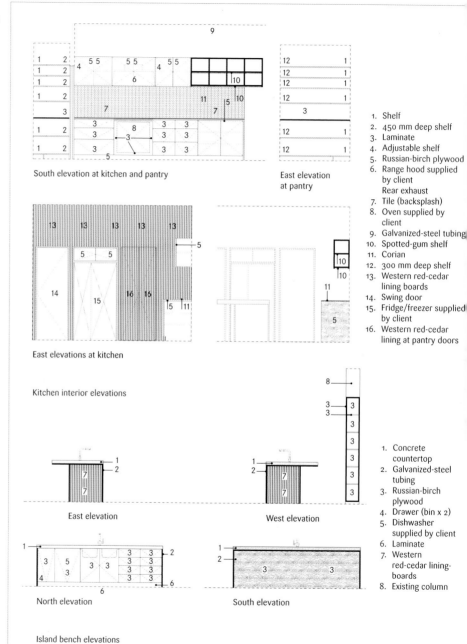

South elevation at kitchen and pantry

East elevation at pantry

East elevations at kitchen

Kitchen interior elevations

1. Shelf
2. 450 mm deep shelf
3. Laminate
4. Adjustable shelf
5. Russian-birch plywood
6. Range hood supplied by client Rear exhaust
7. Tile (backsplash)
8. Oven supplied by client
9. Galvanized-steel tubing
10. Spotted-gum shelf
11. Corian
12. 300 mm deep shelf
13. Western red-cedar lining boards
14. Swing door
15. Fridge/freezer supplied by client
16. Western red-cedar lining at pantry doors

East elevation

West elevation

North elevation

South elevation

Island bench elevations

1. Concrete countertop
2. Galvanized-steel tubing
3. Russian-birch plywood
4. Drawer (bin x 2)
5. Dishwasher supplied by client
6. Laminate
7. Western red-cedar lining-boards
8. Existing column

036

Combine closed and open storage to organize your kitchenware. Open shelving can provide a handy arrangement for utensils used regularly. It can also make your kitchen look less utilitarian and more personal with the display of special items.

The rich grain of the wall cabinets
plays off the stark black floor, which
dramatically contrasts with the white
walls and vanity.

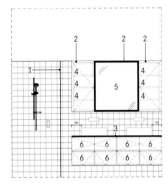

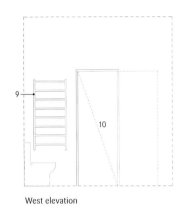

North elevation   East elevation   South elevation   West elevation

Master bathroom interior elevations

1. Glass shower partition   6. White laminate
2. Spotted gum   7. Operable window
3. Corian countertop   8. Tile
4. Adjustable shelf   9. Towel warmer
5. Fixed mirror (recessed) 10. Sliding door

037

A curbless shower with trench drain offers a continuous surface that can be accessible by people in wheelchairs. A minimal glass partition can make a small bathroom feel less confining.

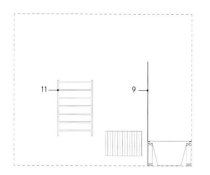

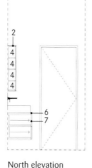

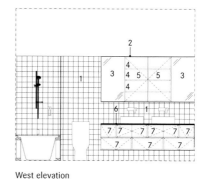

East elevation

North elevation

West elevation

South elevation

Bathroom interior elevation

1. Tile (type 1)
2. Plywood (9 mm)
3. Fixed mirror
4. Adjustable shelf
5. Mirror cabinet
6. Corian countertop
7. White laminate
8. Operable window
9. Glass shower partition
10. Tile (type 2)
11. Towel warmer

038

If space allows, a double-sink vanity offers functionality to a bathroom used by more than one person. They are particularly convenient if there is no additional bathroom available.

039

Pristine finishes and fixtures gleam in an all-white palette that gives this bathroom a fresh and rejuvenating feel.

Hawthorn Residence

Doherty Design Studio
Hawthorn, Victoria, Australia
© Derek Swalwell

The idea behind this project was to breathe new life into a 1980s home by embracing and playing up its heritage yet providing a thoroughly modern aesthetic through custom-made cabinetry, use of color, repetition of pattern, and geometric elements.

Equally important highlights are the revamped stairs, the makeover of the fireplace, a new kitchen/dining area, study nook, refurbished family bathrooms and other wet areas, the refurbished master bedroom, and a new en suite.

In terms of space layout, the design brief required special attention to the redesign of the master bedroom. The existing access was reconfigured to accommodate a generous walk-in closet, and the void area above the house entry hall was reduced to provide floor area for the new en suite.

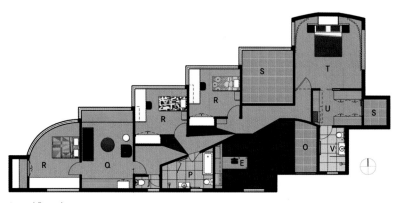

Second floor plan

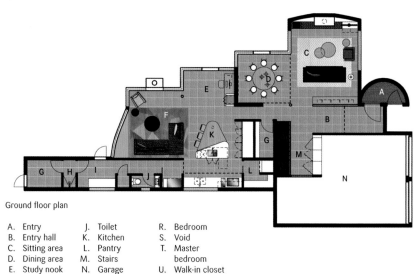

Ground floor plan

A. Entry
B. Entry hall
C. Sitting area
D. Dining area
E. Study nook
F. Living area
G. Storage
H. Pool shower
I. Laundry room

J. Toilet
K. Kitchen
L. Pantry
M. Stairs
N. Garage
O. Void and stairs
P. Bathroom
Q. Home theater

R. Bedroom
S. Void
T. Master bedroom
U. Walk-in closet
V. En suite bathroom

The design brief was a request to retain the home's original features—glass bricks, gray terrazzo floor, pale timber-lined ceilings, and glass-block entry wall.

The kitchen was completely transformed and reenergized to become the central hub of the home. It includes a casual eating area with a custom pedestal-leg table and a breakfast-preparation bar within a walk-in pantry.

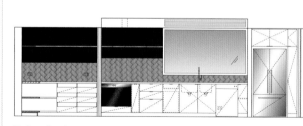

Kitchen elevation

040

If space allows, a two-area
island can provide a section
for food preparation and
allow seating for informal
meals.

041

Rather than applying accent colors to individual walls, try applying it to contiguous walls in order to bring out a volumetric effect.

042

Floor-to-ceiling windows minimize the separation between interior and exterior, integrating the surrounding natural landscape into the living area. The heaviness of a stone-clad fireplace contrasts with the lightness of the overall space, taking center stage.

Fireplace elevation

The makeover of the existing fireplace secured its position as the glamorous focal point of the living area. The new fireplace is set in stone tiles laid in a chevron pattern and folded copper panels that conceal the flue.

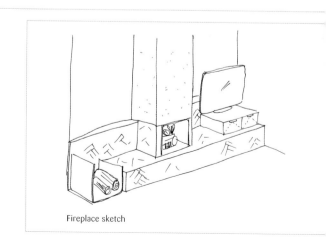

Fireplace sketch

Vintage chairs complete the setting of the retro-style living area dominated by the white-marble and copper-clad fireplace. The golden base of the "egg" chair echoes the copper finish of the fireplace.

The added height of a new bespoke
shelving system on the back wall brings
symmetry and purpose to the room.

043

Revamped stairs include a spectacular feature: bold copper detailing that follows the line of the stair treads and glass balustrades. This upgrade was necessary because the original balustrade did not meet building-code regulations.

The new full-height pivoting timber door
and bespoke headboard in the master
bedroom serve as functional design
statements in keeping with the home's
graphic theme.

Master-bedroom elevation

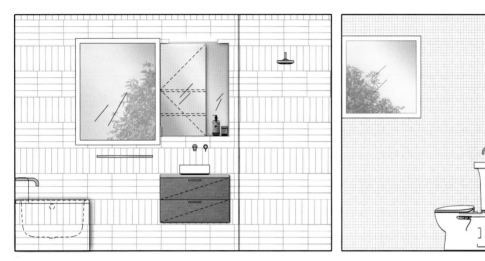

Second floor bathroom elevation

044

Even plain white ceramic
tile can be used creatively.
Explore the possibilities
that different patterns
have to offer, using varying
sizes, creating borders, and
changing the direction of tiles.

Architectural Mews House

Jo Berryman Studio
London, United KIngdom
© Simon Williams

The design of this family mews house, spanning over four floors, pays homage to the distinctive visual and narrative style of American filmmaker Wes Anderson, and to the avant-garde Hollywood Babylon. With a reconfiguration of space, the family home has become architecturally significant, and it revels in the unexpected: dreamy spaces of gleaming surfaces, clean lines, graphic motifs, and earthy finishes.

The property was originally designed with a glazed atrium spanning four floors. It was retained on the top floor but removed below and replaced with a smoked structural glass floor to expand the floor area and allow more light through the various levels.

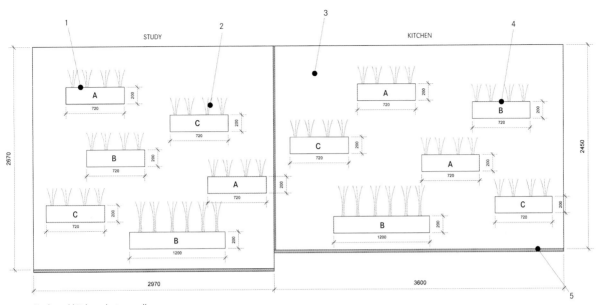

STUDY

KITCHEN

2670

2970

2450

3600

1

2

3

4

5

A   720   200
C   720   200
B   720   200
C   720   200
A   720   200
B   1200   200

A   720   200
C   720   200
A   720   200
B   1200   200
B   720   200
C   720   200

Study and kitchen planters wall

A. Depth: 100 mm
B. Depth: 200 mm
C. Depth: 300 mm

1. Powder-coated zinc planters
2. Painted wall; Farrow & Ball setting plaster
3. Kitchen featured wall; foxed mirror panels in bronze
4. Powder-coated bronze planters
5. Triple-laminated bronze glass

045

Not only do atriums bring light into interior spaces, but they also allow visual connections between different floors, enhancing the extensiveness of these spaces.

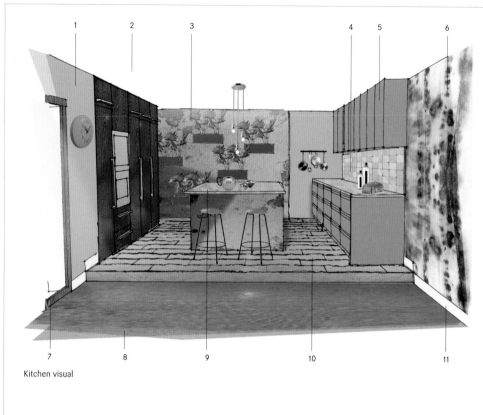

Kitchen visual

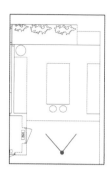

1. Walls: Farrow & Ball "Dead Salmon" color
2. Ceiling: Farrow & Ball "All White" color
3. Wall behind plants and island end: old bronze mirrored panels
4. Splash back: handmade tiles
5. Existing kitchen cabinets: Farrow & Ball "Oval Room Blue"
6. Feature wall: ink-blot wallpaper
7. Existing timber door frame to match new floor
8. Existing dining-room flooring to match new timber floor
9. New countertops: white Carrara marble
10. Kitchen floor: cathedral antiqued limestone
11. Skirting: Farrow & Ball "Cornforth White" color

Farrow & Ball "Dead Salmon" painted walls and muted ceramic backsplash tiles complement the reclaimed-timber flooring and ink-blot wallpaper from **Porter Teleo**.

046

It is important that the kitchen, one of the busiest rooms in a home, gets good lighting. Ambient lighting, which provides an area with overall illumination, needs to be complemented by task lighting directly above work areas.

Living room feature wall

A snug TV corner, a formal seating area with a seventies modular seating arrangement, and a pair of blue velvet chairs complete the trio of spatial pockets, set against the floor-to-ceiling windows and the atrium wall with planters from **Ora Home**.

047

The visual perception we have of a room depends on the selection of colors, how they have been distributed, and in what proportion.

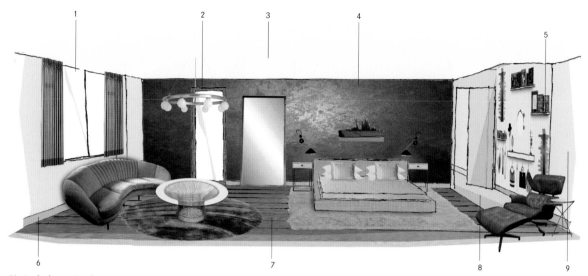

Master bedroom visual

1. Internal window frames: Farrow &
   Ball "Oxford Stone" color
2. Existing timber door frame to match
   new floor
3. Ceiling: Farrow & Ball "Dimitry" color
4. Feature wall: metallic finish by
   specialist
5. Joinery: Farrow & Ball "Cornforth
   White" color
6. Skirting: Farrow & Ball "Oxford
   Stone" color
7. Flooring: engineered floor to match
   reclaimed American barn-wood oak
8. Structural glass floor section and
   pivot door: bronze glass
9. Walls: Farrow & Ball "Cornforth
   White" color

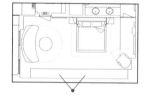

Marco Polo feature walls in metallic
and bronze finishes and a 1950s Italian
curved blue-gray velvet chenille sofa
over a **Tai Ping** bespoke silk circular
rug give the master bedroom a touch of
sophistication.

048

Soft, velvety textiles add a pleasant textural and tactile element to a room. Subdued colors can produce a calming effect. Together they induce a soothing atmosphere that works well for a bedroom.

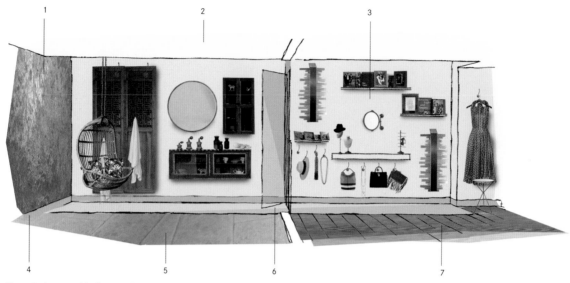

Master bathroom and bedroom wall 2

1. Feature wall: metallic finish by specialist
2. Ceiling: Farrow & Ball "Dimitry" color
3. Walls & joinery: Farrow & Ball " Cornforth White" color
4. Skirting: Farrow & Ball "Oxford Stone"
5. Master bathroom floor: cathedral antiqued limestone
6. Structural glass floor section and pivot door: bronze glass
7. Master bedroom flooring: engineered floor to match reclaimed American barn-wood oak

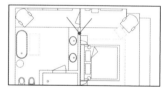

Jo Berryman Studio designed a bespoke display and dressing wall which runs from master bedroom into en suite in a curated arrangement of shelving, circular mirrors, vintage teak cabinetry, and a reused ethnic paneled sculpture which we added hooks for towels and robes to.

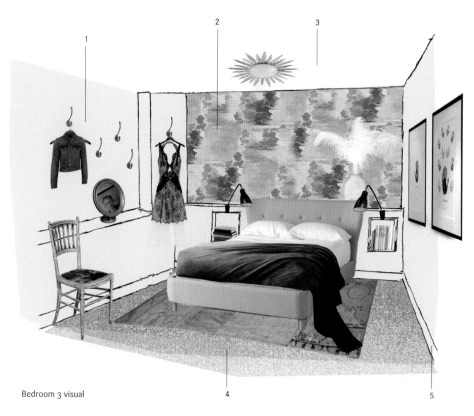

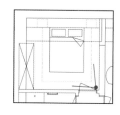

1. Walls: Farrow & Ball "Cornforth White" color
2. Feature wall: "Cloud Toile brown" wallpaper
3. Ceiling: Farrow & Ball "All White" color
4. Floor: velour dove carpet
5. Skirting: Farrow & Ball "Cornforth White" color

Bedroom 3 visual

049

Faux finishes like sponging, color washing, rag rolling, stenciling, and marbleizing bring a unique personal touch to a home.

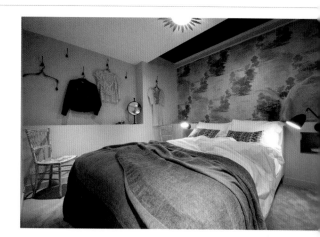

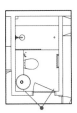

1. Ceiling: Farrow & Ball "All White" color
2. Shower glass screen: bronze glass
3. Walls: iridescent white mosaic tiles
4. Feature wall and shelves: tadelakt by specialist
5. Floor: Fired Earth "Marrakech Sofia" tiles

Basement bathroom visual

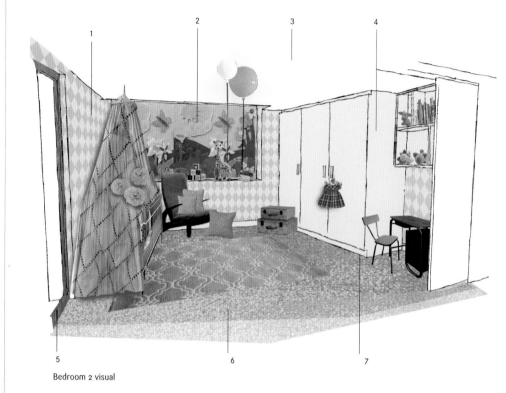

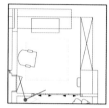

1. Walls: "Harlequin" wallpaper
2. Feature wall: felt landscape
3. Ceiling: Farrow & Ball "All White" color
4. Wardrobe exterior and shelves: Farrow & Ball "Cornforth White" color
5. Existing timber door frame to match new timber floor
6. Floor: velour dove carpet
7. Skirting: Farrow & Ball "Cornforth White" color

Bedroom 2 visual

050

A nursery and little boy's conjoined bedroom is an innovative children's scheme with flexibility for individual and open-plan space.

Redpath

Les Ensembliers

Montreal, Quebec, Canada

© André Rider

Les Ensembliers designed a three-floor, 6,000-square-foot residence that unites three adjoining apartments in a historic former sugar refinery. The architects and designers successfully tackled the challenge of rethinking the original dimensions and use of the industrial building. In joining three separate units, each on a different floor, Les Ensembliers envisioned a coherent new space with a complex personality.

The basic character of each of the zones was defined by a particular treatment of the space, in terms of the design of volumes, the use of materials, and the selection of furniture.

The architectural detailing facilitated the creation of distinctive areas. Paradoxically, the particularities of these different areas were no obstacle to a fluid circulation that connects cozy retreats with spaces designed for exuberant sociability.

Fifth floor plan

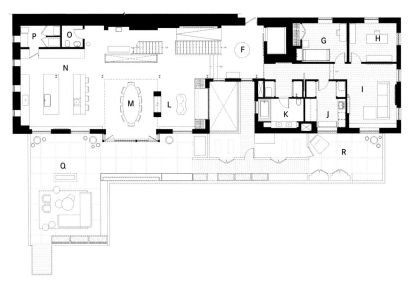

Fourth floor plan

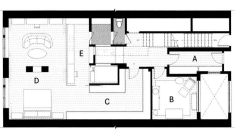

Third floor plan

A. Secondary entrance
B. Office
C. Walk-in closet
D. Master bedroom
E. Master bathroom
F. Entry hall
G. Nursery
H. Bedroom/office
I. Living room
J. Laundry room
K. Children's bathroom
L. Den
M. Dining area
N. Kitchen
O. Powder room
P. Pantry
Q. Main terrace
R. Second terrace
S. Living room/library
T. Guest bathroom
U. Guest room

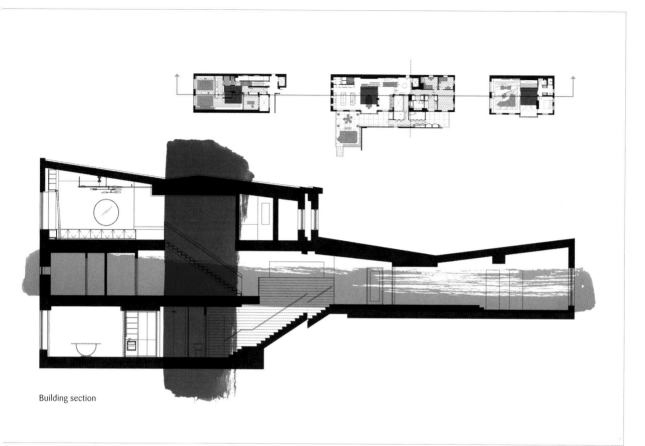

Building section

For the reconfiguration and unification of the three units, the designers opted for two bold architectural statements, one vertical and the other horizontal. The first is a central opening, which creates an atrium linking all three floors. The second is an axis in the form of a bridge and a raised floor linking two staircases.

051

The straight-edged furnishings, the faceted coffee tables, the broken lines of the carpet, the bold colors, and the reflective finishes come together to create vibrant atmosphere.

052

The interior spaces were built as an interplay of contrasts between raw industrial character and a taste for luxury and urban comfort. Everything was designed to highlight the impressive volumes of these old industrial spaces.

053

Visual connections between rooms induce a sense of spaciousness. Circulation elements, such as staircases and corridors, can contribute to this effect when they are placed to create visual axes.

The two low wood walls, framing the stairs toward a lower floor, form a channel indicating the entrance to an intimate haven.

The dining room finds its expression through its stunning central steel fireplace, high ceiling, large oval table, generous windows, and lighting fixtures consisting of small bulbs hanging in a cubic frame made of metal rods.

054

Mirrors and highly polished surfaces alter the perception of a space, making it look larger than it actually is. They can also increase the quantity and quality of a room's light sources.

055

The kitchen responds to a
design approach that focuses
on efficient workflow: the
different tasks are organized
around three minimalist islands,
while all the storage and the
appliances are concealed
behind highly reflective, full-
height cabinet fronts.

056

Nowadays, a well-planned open kitchen is often the true meeting point of a home. A very spacious kitchen can accommodate multiple islands to serve various functions: for instance, for food preparation, cooking, and for serving informal meals.

057

A bathroom mirror can do more than just show one's reflection. Interesting shapes, sizes, and designs can provide a bathroom with character and create a startling focal point.

058

Everything speaks to the embracing comforts of a home: from warm colors and surfaces that are a delight to the touch to the carefully selected furnishings and finishes, such as turquoise silk surfaces, velvet upholstery, and even penny-covered walls!

The master bedroom on the lower
floor expresses luxurious comfort, with
nods to the Asian aesthetics and urban
chic seen in the selection of materials,
finishes, and decorative elements. For
instance, the veins in the fireplace's
Verona marble inspired the choice of
the Japanese painting over the bed.

In the master bathroom, metallic silk curtains provide a flexible separation from the adjacent bedroom. The transparent acrylic legs of the vanity echo the openness and fluidity of the spaces on the upper floors.

Edge

Jenny Martin Design

Cadboro Bay, British Columbia,
Canada

© Joshua Lawrence

This modern home boasts a dynamic interior with large
expanses of glass that let in abundant natural light; high ceilings
that lift heavy steel beams; industrial elements; and hard
angles that harmonize with exposed concrete and minimalist
furnishings. All this rawness is softened by the warm tones
of wood. Views complement the art and are maximized in the
open floor plan. Each room is uniquely its own but designed
with a common theme: modern, spacious, and high-contrast
with simple details executed to perfection.

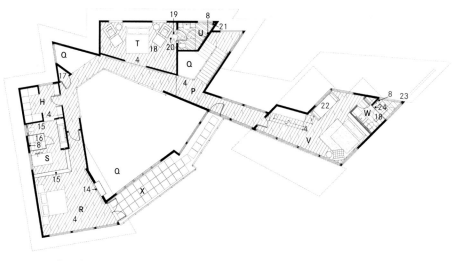

Upper floor plan

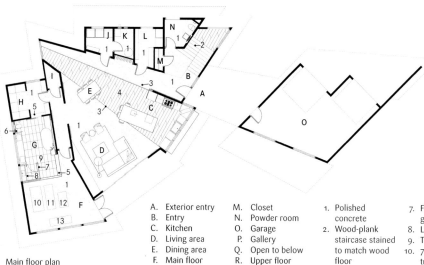

Main floor plan

A.	Exterior entry	M.	Closet
B.	Entry	N.	Powder room
C.	Kitchen	O.	Garage
D.	Living area	P.	Gallery
E.	Dining area	Q.	Open to below
F.	Main floor master bedroom	R.	Upper floor master bedroom
G.	Main floor master en suite	S.	Upper floor master en suite
H.	Master closet	T.	Media room
I.	Linen cabinet	U.	Media en suite
J.	Laundry room	V.	Office
K.	Mechanical room	W.	Office en suite
L.	Pantry	X.	Deck

1. Polished concrete
2. Wood-plank staircase stained to match wood floor
3. Inlaid stainless steel strip
4. Wood floor
5. Polished concrete slab step
6. Cut tile along window wall
7. Floor-to-ceiling glass, no curb
8. Linear drain
9. Tile (type 1)
10. 79" x 36" treadmill
11. 78" x 28" elliptical trainer
12. 48" x 28" stationary bike
13. Yoga mat
14. Dashed line denotes millwork valence
15. Wood-plank step stained to match wood floor
16. Tile (type 2)
17. Washer/dryer
18. Vaulted ceiling
19. Tile (type 3)
20. Tile (type 4)
21. Shower corner squared-off
22. Chaise longue
23. Cut tile along back of shower
24. Tile (type 5)

059

A dynamic plan organization
is enhanced by a combination
of two floor materials that
differentiate areas.

High-reaching ceilings and light walls provide the canvas for this stunning entertainment kitchen overlooking the ocean. Color-blocking and high-contrast elements pop in the abundance of natural light. Heavy beams pair with stainless steel and are lightened with white quartz, layered lighting, and oiled oak flooring.

Industrial elements pair with large-scale millwork yet are proportionate to the grand space. In the kitchen, a **Western Window Systems** folding window above the sink makes the countertop a bar open to the outside.

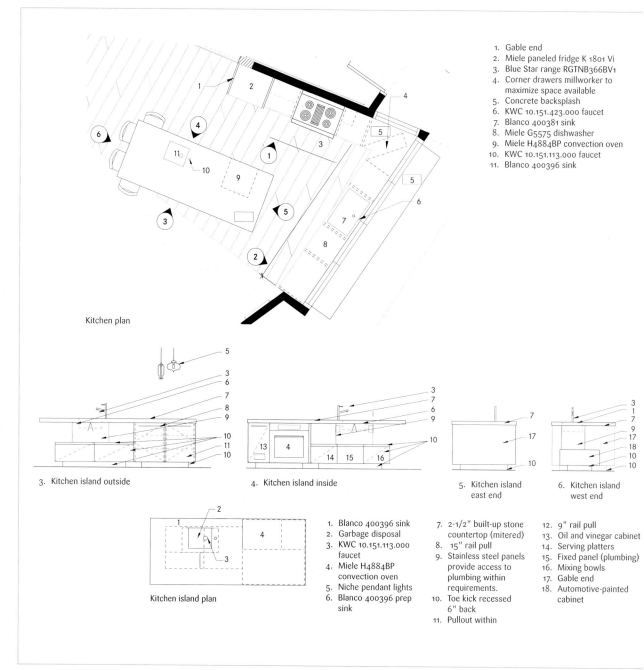

Kitchen plan

1. Gable end
2. Miele paneled fridge K 1801 Vi
3. Blue Star range RGTNB366BV1
4. Corner drawers millworker to maximize space available
5. Concrete backsplash
6. KWC 10.151.423.000 faucet
7. Blanco 400381 sink
8. Miele G5575 dishwasher
9. Miele H4884BP convection oven
10. KWC 10.151.113.000 faucet
11. Blanco 400396 sink

3. Kitchen island outside

4. Kitchen island inside

5. Kitchen island east end

6. Kitchen island west end

Kitchen island plan

1. Blanco 400396 sink
2. Garbage disposal
3. KWC 10.151.113.000 faucet
4. Miele H4884BP convection oven
5. Niche pendant lights
6. Blanco 400396 prep sink

7. 2-1/2" built-up stone countertop (mitered)
8. 15" rail pull
9. Stainless steel panels provide access to plumbing within requirements.
10. Toe kick recessed 6" back
11. Pullout within

12. 9" rail pull
13. Oil and vinegar cabinet
14. Serving platters
15. Fixed panel (plumbing)
16. Mixing bowls
17. Gable end
18. Automotive-painted cabinet

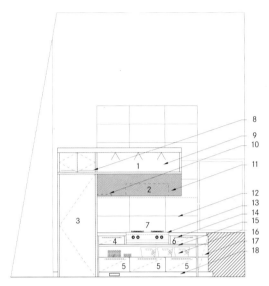

1. Kitchen northeast wall

2. Kitchen southeast wall

1. Open shelf
2. Zephyr Monsoon 1 hood
3. Miele K1801 Vi paneled fridge
4. Utensil drawer
5. Pot drawer
6. Spice drawer
7. Blue Star RGTNB366BV1 range
8. 9" rail pull

9. Open shelving for display
10. Open shelf behind range surround
11. Faux finished range surround to be determined; corners to be mitered; all exposed edges to be finished; channel to be routered out of bottom of slab to allow for LED light strip

12. Engraved basalt backsplash
13. 2½" built-up edge countertop (mitered)
14. 15" rail pull
15. 1½" gables, typical
16. Open storage with false panel recessed as far back as possible

17. Corner drawers for cooking utensils, cups, and mugs
18. Toe kick to be recessed back 6" vacuum kick to be added
19. 6" rail pull; pullout to appear as separate drawers

20. Garbage/recycle
21. Tilt drawer
22. Miele G5575 dishwasher
23. Dishware drawer
24. Drawers to be cut out to allow for a P-trap
25. Blanco 400381 sink
26. KWC 10.151.423.000 faucet

060

A floating vanity, sliding mirrors, and barn door evoke movement, while views through the windows offer art and texture.

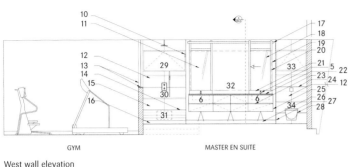

West wall elevation

GYM MASTER EN SUITE

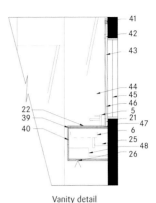

Vanity detail

Plan

Main floor master en suite

East wall elevation

1. Steam
2. Blu Bathworks TD118, TSP860S, TE510 shower parts
3. Floor-to-ceiling glass, seamless shower surround, no curb
4. Sliding fabric panels
5. Aquabrass KG514 faucet
6. Kohler K-2882-0 sink
7. Duravit 253309 toilet
8. Wall furred out to accommodate horizontal niche
9. Aquabrass B0016 freestanding bathtub
10. Additional hand-shower holder mounted to glass
11. Stationary mirror
12. Provenza Q-Stone
13. Quartz strip for glass and tile to butt into

14. Floating teak slat bench with removable top; steam unit to be hidden within
15. Tile detail to wrap onto pony wall within shower only
16. Provenza Q-Stone toe kick
17. Horizontal flat oil-rubbed bronze bar to suspend mirrors
18. Sliding mirror on track
19. Dashed line denotes window behind mirrors
20. Flat oil-rubbed bronze mirror frame to hang from bar above
21. Flat oil-rubbed bronze bars to form backsplashes
22. ¾" thick countertop
23. Integrated handle
24. Top of furred-out wall
25. Floating vanity; please ensure P-trap is enclosed within cabinetry

26. Under-cabinet lighting
27. Floor-to-ceiling glass partition
28. Wall-mount toilet; wall to be furred out to accommodate tank
29. 4' 2-1/4" x 2' 0" window
30. Blu Bathworks TD118, TSP850S, TE510 shower parts
31. Steam
32. 8' 1" x 3' 10" new window
33. 3' 0" x 2' 0" new window
34. Duravit 253309 toilet
35. Drywalled niche; please construct as deep as possible
36. Aquabrass tub filler 27518
37. Floating teak shelf to wrap around tub
38. Bulkhead to be constructed and painted to match wall if plumbing is visible below shelf
39. Reveal

40. Fixed panel
41. Vertical flat oil-rubbed bronze bars to wrap over top of horizontal bar to suspend mirrors
42. Top of mirror surround flat-oil rubbed bronze bar
43. Left mirror to be stationary, right mirror to slide across entire width of vanity
44. Seamless glass shower surround
45. Window behind mirrors
46. Mirrors framed with flat oil-rubbed bronze bars
47. Routered channel for sliding mirror track
48. Drawer to be cut out around P-trap

061

The steps from the bedroom up to the bathroom provide a level of separation between the two areas, while a visual connection is maintained, creating an open atmosphere.

The vanity, soaking tub, shower, and windows echo the architecture's linear elements and are a testimony to workmanship quality and attention to detail.

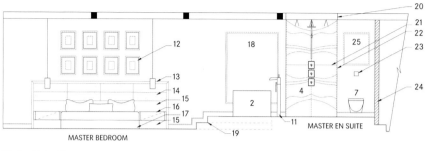

West wall elevation

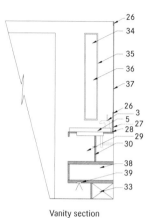

Vanity section

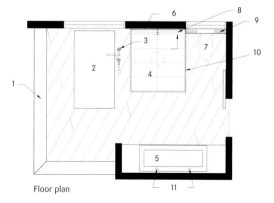

East wall elevation

Upper floor master en suite

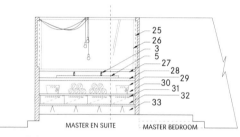

Floor plan

1. Wood-plank step stained to match wood-floor
2. WETSTYLE BC10 bathtub
3. Hansgrohe 10456001 chrome tub filler
4. Blu Bathworks TD118, TSP860S, TE510 shower parts
5. WETSTYLE VCS 60T trough sink
6. Marble slab
7. Duravit 253309 toilet
8. Linear drain
9. Furred out wall
10. 1 ½" quartz strip 1/8" higher than tile in shower and wood floor to act as transition strip and for glass to butt in to
11. Hansgrohe 10111001 chrome faucet
12. Art
13. 2" x 2" mitered cap to capture panels
14. Fabric panels
15. Millwork panels
16. Built-in bedside table
17. Bed frame
18. 4' 2" x 6' 0" new window
19. Stairs shifted 10" into bedroom to allow for tub
20. Bulkhead to extend into room above shower surround
21. Book-matched-marble slab
22. Floor-to-ceiling seamless glass shower partition
23. Flush valve
24. Entire wall mount toilet wall to be furred out to accommodate tank
25. Recessed panels of light refer to detail
26. Flat oil-rubbed bronze mirror surround
27. ¾" backsplash polished top edge
28. Built-up 2½" countertop (mitered)
29. Open shelving
30. False panel to hide P-traps
31. 10" sandcast
32. Floating millwork
33. Toe kick recessed 1' back to allow for easy cleaning; painted to match walls
34. Ventilation hole may be required at top of niche
35. ½" flat oil-rubbed bronze frame to capture edge of frosted glass
36. Recessed niche: LED strip light behind frosted glass; frosted glass to sit flush with face of drywall
37. Mirror
38. Drawer
39. Under-cabinet lighting

062

Diagonal hardwood flooring is simply personal preference. Perhaps it is not very common because installing it diagonally involves more work and requires a higher waste factor than orthogonally installed wood flooring.

Bletchley Loft

Jodie Cooper Design

Perth, Western Australia,
Australia

© The Rural Building Company

The design brief for Bletchley Loft called for the creation of
open but defined living areas. This was achieved through
elements such as the kitchen island and the central
entertainment and display unit, which demarcate the areas
without interfering with a natural circulation flow. Aesthetically,
the design blends retro and rustic styles against a backdrop of
neutral colors. Antique Asian furniture and artifacts, jeweled
colored ikat cushions, and Turkish patterned rugs add color,
pattern, and texture, giving the interior multicultural vitality.

Second floor plan

Ground floor plan

A. Porch
B. Entry hall
C. Living area
D. Dining area
E. Kitchen
F. Alfresco dining
   and garden

G. Bedroom
H. Bathroom
I. Powder room
J. Storage
K. Home office
L. Laundry room
M. Garage

N. Void
O. Master bedroom
P. Activity room
Q. Master bathroom
R. Dressing room

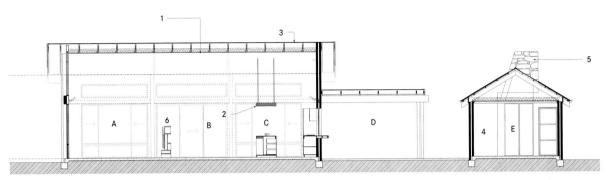

Longitudinal building section

A. Living area
B. Dining area
C. Kitchen
D. Outdoor dining area
E. Bedroom

1. Raking plasterboard ceiling lining
    to underside of rafters
2. Suspended canopy
3. Colorbond roof
4. Full height mirror sliding door
5. Carved feature wall or similar
6. Freestanding TV unit

There are two defined zones in the home, one being the large open plan living area including galley style kitchen and upstairs master retreat, and the second being the three bedrooms and activity room arranged around an outdoor dining area.

The open-plan living area with its high-raked ceiling required special design elements to add to the room's functionality. These elements pair with the generous proportions of the space to achieve a lofty and airy feel.

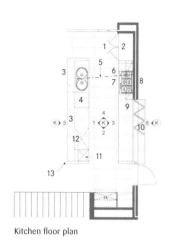

Kitchen floor plan

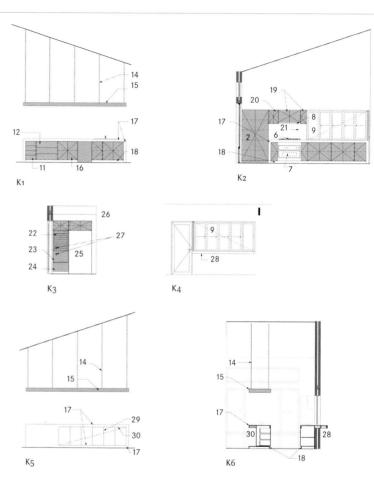

K1

K2

K3

K4

K5

K6

Kitchen elevations

1. 4 x 450 cm shelves at 400 cm
2. Laminate pantry
3. Laminate back
4. Dishwasher
5. Conduit in slab by plumber
6. Gas HP
7. Gas HP with UBO
8. Hood above
9. Bi-fold door
10. Exterior breakfast bar
11. Bank of four drawers
12. Three-pot drawers
13. Canopy over island bench; size to full extends length of island bench
14. S/S hollow tube fixed from ceiling to canopy (tube also contains electrical cabling for down light within canopy)
15. Suspended canopy over island bench with down lights
16. Bin cabinet
17. 100 mm thick fascia surround to kitchen bench top (to continue down the side)
18. 100 mm high recessed kickboard
19. Power point to hood at 1800 mm above finished floor
20. Overhead cabinets
21. Tiled backsplash
22. Appliance garage
23. Microwave recess
24. Pot drawer
25. Refrigerator recess
26. 300 mm deep overhead cabinet
27. GPO at 1050 mm above finished floor for appliance garage; GPO at 800 mm above finished floor for microwave
28. 100 mm high overhang to outdoors
29. Divide laminate back into six equal panels
30. 300 mm overhang open to laminate back

Lighting is functional and aesthetically pleasing. Wall-mounted up-lights ensure that there is enough reflected light from the white ceilings, while a suspended bulkhead provides task lighting for the kitchen island.

The floor-to-ceiling glass wall above the living area is inspired by the boxy look of a foreman's office. The open-tread staircase to the second floor reveals a spacious master bedroom with a beautifully appointed en suite bathroom and large walk-in closet.

063

In the master bedroom, the calming décor and the soft ambient light filtered through the sheer curtains indicate a secluded retreat.

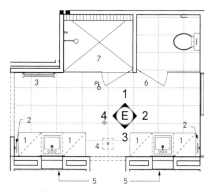

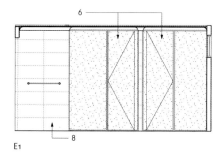

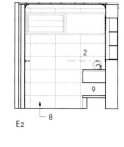

En suite floor plan

1. Drawer
2. Towel ring
3. Towel rail
4. Ceiling-mounted fan
5. Shelf built into wall behind mirror
6. Obscure glazed 750 mm wide pivot door with obscure fixed glazed panel
7. Hobless shower
8. 300 mm x 600 mm tiles to full height (underside of cornice)
9. Shelf
10. Through to walk-in closet
11. Inset basin
12. 250 mm high tiled plinth
13. 600 mm wide mirror with 230 mm deep shelves behind; mirror projecting 10 mm off wall with 20 mm deep finger-grip access

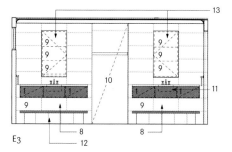

En suite elevations

064

If space allows, a "his" and "her" vanity provide for separate areas for each—the ultimate in luxury bathroom design.

065

Good lighting is critical in bathroom design. Just like kitchens, bathrooms require different types of illumination: ambient lighting to provide overall illumination, and task lighting on specific areas, such as the vanity.

738 Broadway

**Andres Escobar/Escobar
Design by Lemay**

Manhattan, New York,
United States

© Robert Lowell

The Broadway McKenna Building, originally a Greenwich Village industrial warehouse, was extensively remodeled to accommodate modern apartments adapted to the neighborhood's new upbeat lifestyle. At the same time, the design concept allows the McKenna Building to proudly remind us of its industrial origin.

Wide-open areas, high ceilings, large windows, and light tones gracefully combine to accentuate the remarkable spatial qualities of the living areas. An Italian Calacatta marble fireplace is the focal point in a design scheme that is a fine balance between opulence and sobriety.

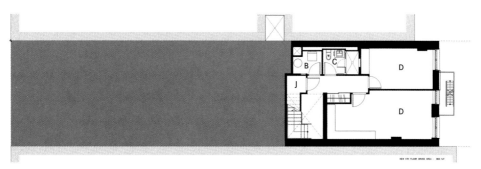

Fourth floor plan

Third floor plan

Second floor plan

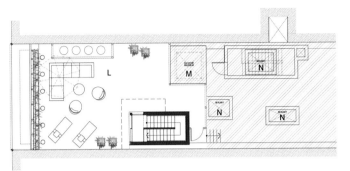

A. Entry hall	I. Elevator
B. Laundry room	J. Closet
C. Bathroom	K. ADA Bathroom
D. Bedroom	compliant
E. Master bedroom	L. Roof terrace
F. Master bathroom	M. Elevator bulkhead
G. Kitchen	N. Skylight
H. Living/dining room	

Roof terrace plan

Fifth floor plan

The building includes two 2,400-square-foot and one 3,200-square-foot lofts spread out on its two first floors. It is topped with a 2,400-square-foot penthouse featuring a 900-square-foot private terrace.

066

The seventeen-foot-long fireplace is emphasized by concealing its top into the dropped ceiling and cove lighting. This design detail wraps the fireplace, creating a strong sense of height and vertical continuity.

The kitchen is equipped with **Miele** and **Sub-Zero** appliances concealed within quality custom-designed Italian cabinets. The white island ties in with the white walls and ceiling.

067

Cove lighting is a form of indirect illumination suitable for ambient lighting. The light is directed toward the ceiling and reflected back to the room to achieve an evenly lit space. Additional task-light sources may be required.

The master bathroom, clad in Calacatta marble and textured **Porcelanosa** "Cubica" floor tiles, feature an overflow bathtub, cove lighting complemented with recessed can lights, and a mirror TV.

Reminiscent of the Soho lofts in New York, the Saint Martins Lofts occupy the top four floors of the former Central Saint Martins College of Art and Design. The original building features a mix of arts-and-crafts and modern architectural elements. The design of this renovated apartment injects new life into the existing building with outstanding architectural features. In keeping with 19 Greek Street's philosophy, the design promotes sustainability, social design, and up-cycling, featuring unique pieces by Nina Tolstrup of Studio Mama and Beirut-based Karen Chekerdjian.

Saint Martins Loft

19 Greek Street

London, United Kingdom

© Marina Castagna,
   Jamie McGregor Smith

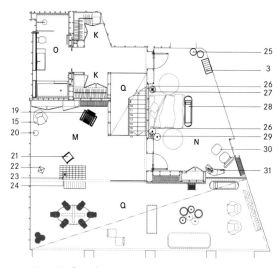

Mezzanine floor plan

A. Entry hall
B. Guest bathroom
C. Plant
D. Coat closet
E. Hub closet
F. Kitchen
G. Dining area
H. Living area
I. Laundry room
J. Bathroom
K. Dressing room
L. Bedroom
M. Home office
N. Master bedroom
O. Master bathroom
P. Open to above
Q. Open to below

1. Wing bench
2. Endless Series elephant skin table
3. Breg Hanssen framed cabinet
4. Nina Tolstrup Re-Imagined tall chairs
5. Endless Series oval flat line dining table
6. Kami lights
7. Saj table
8. Things

9. Elephant chair
10. Wing side tables
11. Daybed
12. Composition of Air
13. Flos aim lights
14. Petite Vague
15. Classic recycled armchair
16. Composition of Cookie Paper, Yoyo, Derbakeh
17. Jaime Hayon Beetley sofa
18. David David Re-Imagined Daybed with hex print
19. Papillion chair
20. Melting pot side table
21. 9.5° chair
22. Kite stool
23. Book table
24. Timber anglepoise table lamp
25. Corks
26. Karen Chekerdjian yo-yo stool/ side table
27. Mass Produced individualism
28. Nina Tolstrup Re-Imagined daybed
29. Derbakeh by Karen Chekerdjian
30. Nina Tolstrup Re-Imagined low chair
31. Karen Chekerdjian Ikebana mirror

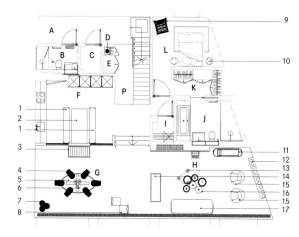

Lower floor plan: option 1

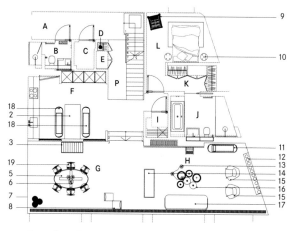

Lower floor plan: option 2

068

An entryway can make a bold design statement that introduces the style of the whole interior. It is, after all, the first area that one finds upon entering a home.

The generously proportioned living spaces feature original steel-framed windows and high ceilings, maintaining the original architectural character of the former Saint Martins School of Art and Design.

View of preexisting conditions

Artist's rendition of living and dining areas

069

Tall walls can be utilized as extended areas for storage and display. Access to areas beyond reach from the floor is the only issue, but it can be easily resolved with a ladder that can slide across the length of the wall.

Saint Martins Loft **195**

The kitchen, the bathrooms, laundry room, guest bedroom, and closets are concentrated below the mezzanine, so as to leave the bright, spacious area along the window wall for daytime activities.

Artist's rendition of kitchen

070

The studio on the mezzanine is a sparsely furnished space that lends itself to a variety of activities, promoting the concept of flexible space.

The simple yet eye-catching staircase
to the mezzanine makes a strong design
statement in keeping with the clarity
of the space layout and the selection
of contemporary furnishings and
decorations.

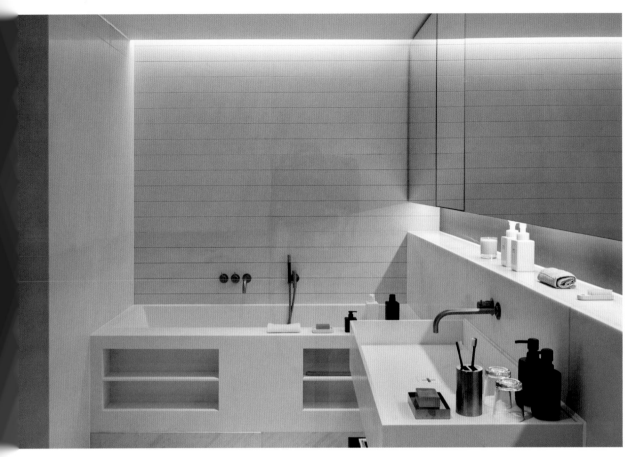

071

Polymer-resin bathroom fixtures can be cast to any shape and design. They are smooth and warm to the touch and are easy to clean and maintain.

House MM

Menichetti+Caldarelli

Gubbio, Italy

© Paolo Tosti

The design concept of this two-level apartment focuses on the articulation of vertical and horizontal planes, making up a strong geometric composition based on the principles of visual balance. The material and color palette is limited to the use of white finishes, light-colored concrete, and accents of burnished brass on key organizational elements. Light is used as an integral design element to further enhance the volumetric character of the composition, adding subtle nuance to all the surfaces.

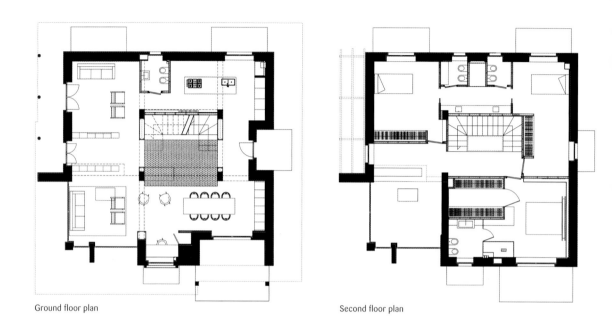

Ground floor plan

Second floor plan

The different functions of the apartment
are organized around a central staircase
and burnished-brass fireplace under a
dropped ceiling of the same material.
Two bookcases of different heights are
secondary organizational elements.

072

Used as space dividers—as opposed to placed against a wall—bookshelves can be accessed from both sides, which makes them more functional.

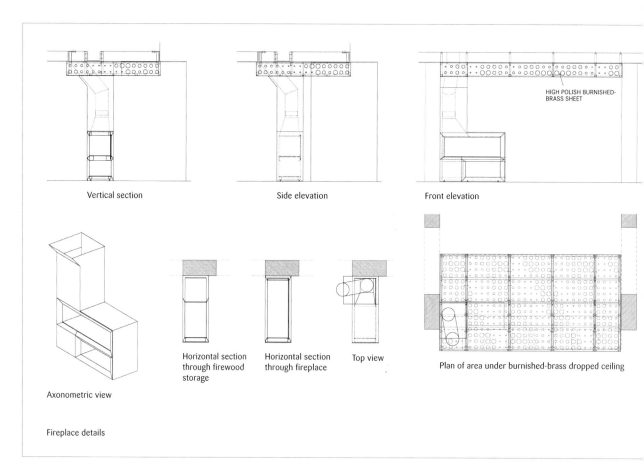

Vertical section

Side elevation

Front elevation

HIGH POLISH BURNISHED-BRASS SHEET

Axonometric view

Horizontal section through firewood storage

Horizontal section through fireplace

Top view

Plan of area under burnished-brass dropped ceiling

Fireplace details

The highlight of this project is a custom-made fireplace and wood box made of brass sheet and topped by a dropped ceiling made of perforated burnished-brass panels. This ceiling feature is actually a large light fixture that emits light through holes of different diameters.

The fireplace and perforated brass dropped ceiling occupy a central location on the lower floor of the apartment. These elements mark the access to the second floor via a staircase that turns from concrete to wood, demonstrating a dematerialization design concept.

073

The design of the apartment is a study on balance: light and dark, low and high, vertical and horizontal. All these elements come together to achieve a serene and comfortable environment.

074

Etched glass—also, frosted glass—provides obscuration and vision control without compromising light levels. Etched glass actually diffuses light, creating a unique soothing feeling.

075

Patterned tiles are not new, but mixing different patterns seems to be a trend that has broken mainly into contemporary bathroom and kitchen design, expanding the planning possibilities of tile work.

This house has two souls for its two levels. The ground floor is bright and open to the outside, accommodating typical living functions—a living room, a kitchen, bedrooms, and bathrooms. The underground floor is conceived as an intimate entertainment area, just as suitable for one person's enjoyment as it is for small gatherings; in contrast with the floor above, it is an enclosed and quiet zone, a place where one can find a moment of solitude, away from the everyday routine of the floor above.

Luna House

Buratti Architetti

Nerviano, Italy

© Marcello Mariana

The lower floor is conceived like a contemporary hypogeum, with polished concrete surfaces instead of stone. It is a cavernous yet inviting space, where a changing colored light plays a central role, transforming the atmosphere.

The pool is isolated from the rest of the space by floor-to-ceiling glass panels, reflecting light to create an atmosphere that takes occupants of this space to a fantastic world.

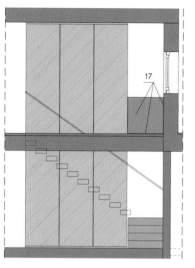
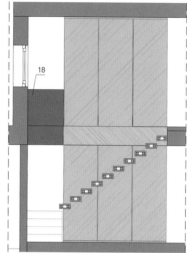
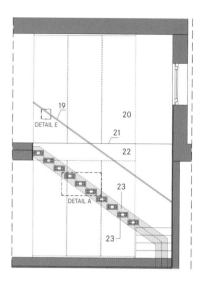

Staircase sections

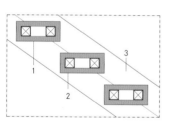

Detail A

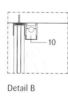

Detail B   Detail C

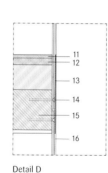

Detail D

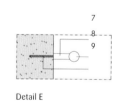

Detail E

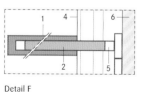

Detail F

Stair details

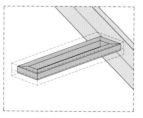

Axonometric view of tread and stringer attachment detail

1. Wood-cladded steps
2. 60 x 60 x 3 steel tubing
3. Two 50 x 150 x 4 mm tubular stringer attached to masonry wall
4. Wall finish
5. Steel tube welded to stringer
6. Masonry wall
7. 14 mm diameter brushed steel
8. 25 mm diameter brushed steel
9. 8-10 mm threaded rod
10. Linear LED lamp
11. Wood flooring
12. Subfloor
13. Pink mirror
14. Mounting screws
15. Concrete slab
16. Pink glass
17. Guardrail, wall cladding, and flooring in black steel
18. Black steel guardrail
19. Brushed stainless steel tubular handrail
20. Painted wall
21. Finished floor in brushed stainless steel
22. Resined wall
23. Steel-framed steps cladded in solid wood

A cantilevered open-tread staircase connects the two floors. Its weightless nature is emphasized by colored glass panels that give the light around the staircase a soft pink tint.

In keeping with the design's focus on color and materiality, black steel spans from floor to ceiling and integrates a fireplace, shelves, and TV screen.

The whole ground floor is designed as a composition of interconnected spaces, only set apart by moveable panels.

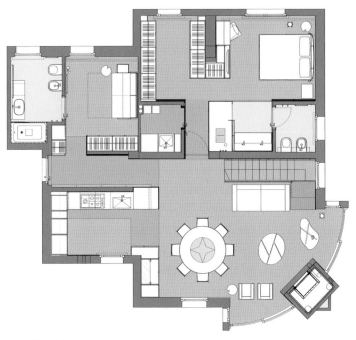

Upper floor plan

Lower floor plan

076

A stainless steel kitchen isn't necessarily cold. Combined with wood, the reflective surfaces take on the warm tones. Lighting needs to be carefully designed to minimize glare.

077

Tinted glass has great visual appeal. As a building material, glass features innovative technology that meets safety requirements. Because it's tinted, it is obviously visible, and is therefore a suitable room divider that does not block light.

078

Texture, like color, can influence the perception of space. For instance, matte surfaces truly define the limits of a room, whereas high-gloss finishes make a space look less tangible because of the reflectivity factor, which tends to visually expand the space.

Greenwich Village Town House

SAS \ Solomonoff Architecture Studio

Manhattan, New York, United States

© David Joseph

A nationally landmarked Greek-revival building constructed in 1868 was upgraded to accommodate a growing family and a large collection of contemporary art. The ground floor, which for some time was used as a hair salon, was too exposed to the street and therefore a privacy issue. The open plan of this floor made possible the creation of a site-specific art piece that would respond to the owners' interest in art and, at the same time, provide a private area for the children to play and guests to stay.

Building front elevation

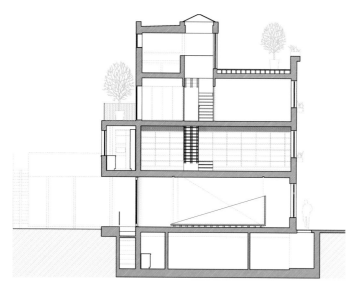

Building section

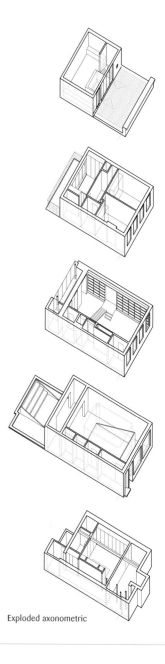

Exploded axonometric

079

Lights inside the **Corian** handrail provide additional safety and complement the minimal design of the top floor under a large skylight.

The sturdy formality of the existing building informed the upper, more private floors, which were reconfigured to maximize art display, facilitate entertaining, and cater to the growing family's needs.

080

The bathroom transmits an understated and timeless elegance through the use of various shades of white. The veining of Carrara marble adds subtle visual texture.

This four-story town house maintains its original elegant detailing and is complemented by customized items, including doors, windows, shelves, sinks, and a staircase, as well as various pieces of cabinetry for the kitchen, living room, and bathrooms. Exquisite materials and finishes—rustic timber floors, polished concrete, and tadelakt surfaces—serve as backdrop to a fantastic collection of vintage furniture, light fixtures, and artwork. The design stands out for its clean lines, color palette of muted colors, and rich materials, which combined achieve a sophisticated and refined aesthetic.

Graham Road

Waind Gohil Architects and Casa Botelho

London, United Kingdom

© Juliet Murphy

The owners of the town house purchased the top two floors first. Then came the two lower floors a few years later. The refurbishing of the building resulted in the creation of a three-story home with a ground floor extension, while the basement was turned into a separate two-bedroom unit.

Third floor plan

1. Polished screed	A. Communal hall
2. Electrical meters	B. Living area
3. Washing machine	C. Dining area
4. Dishwasher	D. Kitchen
5. Refrigerator/freezer	E. Study
6. Oven	F. Bathroom
7. Mirror	G. Bedroom
8. Hardwood floor	H. Hall
9. Cooktop	I. Powder room
10. Wine cooler	J. Terrace
11. Microwave / oven / warming drawer	K. Rear garden
	L. Outdoor dining
12. Reconstituted stone	M. BBQ area
13. Belfast sink	N. Outbuilding
14. Washing machine and pump dryer stacked	O. Seating area
	P. En suite bathroom
15. Tile	Q. Dressing room
16. Radiator	R. Landing
17. Hardwood decking	S. Master bedroom
18. Stone	

Second floor plan

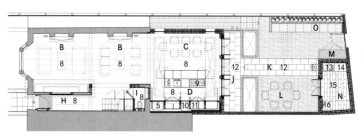

Ground floor plan. Garden

Basement floor plan

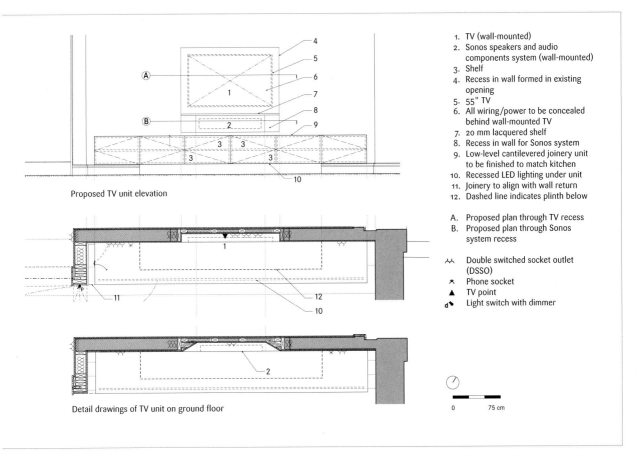

Proposed TV unit elevation

1. TV (wall-mounted)
2. Sonos speakers and audio components system (wall-mounted)
3. Shelf
4. Recess in wall formed in existing opening
5. 55" TV
6. All wiring/power to be concealed behind wall-mounted TV
7. 20 mm lacquered shelf
8. Recess in wall for Sonos system
9. Low-level cantilevered joinery unit to be finished to match kitchen
10. Recessed LED lighting under unit
11. Joinery to align with wall return
12. Dashed line indicates plinth below

A. Proposed plan through TV recess
B. Proposed plan through Sonos system recess

ᴧᴧ Double switched socket outlet (DSSO)
ⵝ Phone socket
▲ TV point
ᑯ Light switch with dimmer

Detail drawings of TV unit on ground floor

0   75 cm

The entertainment center is fully integrated into the space, with a large flat-screen mounted into a niche. A long, low wood cabinet acts as a shelf for the niche, anchoring it to the dark floor.

081

Original architectural features, such as fireplaces and brick walls, offer a sense of history. Light fixtures and mirrors add dimension and a sense of opulence.

The kitchen is an area of high contrast: the clean lines and smooth surfaces of the wall unit and island are a counterpoint to the roughness of the brick wall opposite. Two crystal chandeliers hang above a long table. When lit, they pick up the warm tones of the brick.

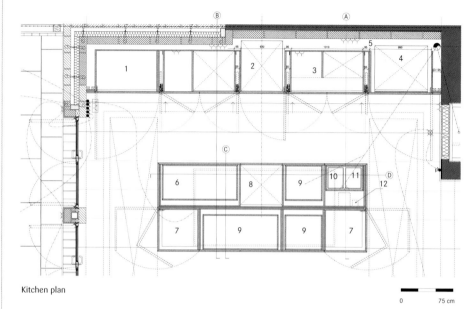

Kitchen plan

1. Larder
2. Tefcold TFW360-2 dual compartment wine cooler
3. Tea point
4. Liebherr, PremiumPlus BioFresh NoFrost fridge/freezer, ECBN 5066
5. Service void to the rear
6. Utensils drawer
7. Two-sided corner-access storage
8. 60 cm Bosch ActiveWater SMV69T30GB dishwasher
9. Pullout storage
10. Recycling bin
11. General waste bin
12. Water dispenser hot tank including Dornbracht 1289097090 filter

0   75 cm

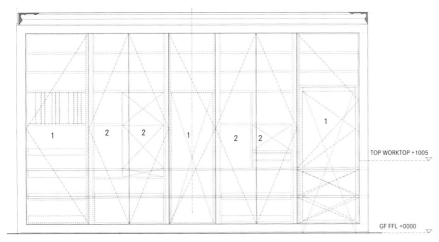

Full-height storage unit elevation (sliding pivot doors closed)

1. Hinged doors
2. Sliding pivot door

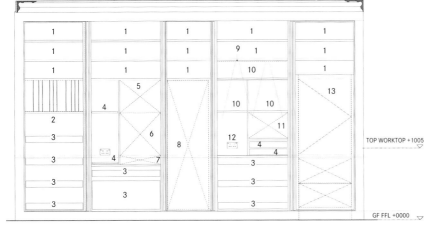

Full-height storage unit elevation (sliding pivot doors open)

1. Shelf
2. Vertical adjustable storage
3. Pullout storage
4. Pullout shelf
5. 60 cm Fisher & Paykel OM36NDXB1 built-in combination microwave oven
6. 60 cm Fisher & Paykel OB60SL11DEPX11-function p yrolytic oven
7. 60 cm Fisher & Paykel WB60SDEB1 warming drawer
8. Tefcold TFW360-2 dual-compartment winw cooler
9. LED strip lighting
10. Narrow shelf
11. Miele Nespresso CVA6431
12. Tea point
13. Liebherr PremiumPlus BioFresh NoFrost fridge/freezer, ECBN 5066

TOP WORKTOP +1005

GF FFL +0000

0   75 cm

Align

1. Decorative concrete works
2. Tonk strips
3. Shelf
4. Extractor (in elevation)
5. 510 x 405 mm Dornbracht 38050000 undermounted sink water unit
6. Pullout storage
7. Dornbracht 1289097090 water dispenser hot tank including filter (behind)
8. Barazza B_Ambient 1KBAS12 ceiling cooktop hood module 120 (concealed within joinery)
9. LED strip lighting
10. Requirement for a 15 mm ventilation gap located at the top and bottom of the kitchen border
11. Tea point
12. Pull out shelf
13. Two narrow pullout shelves
14. Service void to the rear

Top worktop +1005

GF FFL +0000

Detail section A

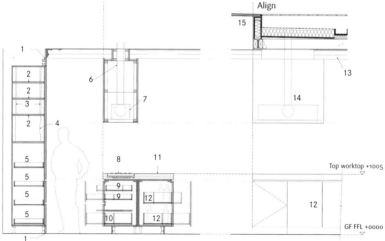

Align

1. Requirement for a 15 mm ventilation gap located at the top and bottom of the kitchen border
2. Shelf
3. Tonk strips
4. Vertical adjustable storage
5. Pullout shelf
6. Exhaust duct to exit through roof
7. B_Ambient ceiling cooktop hood module 120 Barazza, 1KBAS12
8. 115 cm Barazza LAB 1PLB3TI flush and built-in cooktop
9. Cutlery drawer
10. Utensils drawer
11. Decorative concrete works
12. Pullout storage
13. Cornice (beyond)
14. Extractor (in elevation); module shown dashed within

Top worktop +1005

GF FFL +0000

Detail section B

Detail elevation through extractor unit

Detail sections through island and full-height storage unit

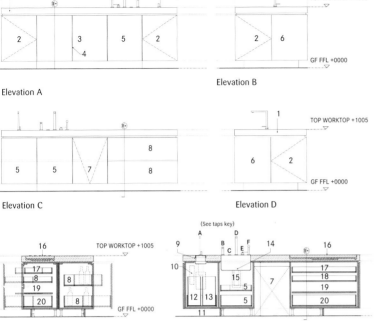

Elevation A

Elevation B

TOP WORKTOP +1005

GF FFL +0000

Elevation C

Elevation D

TOP WORKTOP +1005

GF FFL +0000

Section C

Section D

TOP WORKTOP +1005

GF FFL +0000

1. Decorative concrete works
2. Two-side corner-access storage
3. 1200 mm pullout storage
4. Rout in pullout door
5. 600 mm pullout storage
6. Fixed panel
7. 60 cm Bosch ActiveWater SMV69T30GB
8. 1200 mm pullout storage
9. 210 mm x 405 mm Dornbracht 38001000 undermounted strainer water unit
10. Dornbracht 1289097090 water dispenser hot tank including filter
11. Pullout bin storage above
12. General waste bin
13. Recycling bin
14. 510 mm x 405 mm Dornbracht 38050000 undermounted sinkwater unit
15. InSinkErator Evolution Excel Excel garbage disposal
16. 115 cm Barazza LAB 1PLB3TI built-in cooktop
17. Additional pullout storage
18. Cutlery drawer
19. Pullout shelf
20. Utensil drawer

Taps key Dornbracht:
A: 1785168o hot and cold water dispenser
B: 82437970 integrated washing-up liquid dispenser
C: 10714970 air switch (control button) for controlling waste disposal
D, E: 3280068o two-hole mixer with individual rosettes,
F : 27714970 rinsing spray set

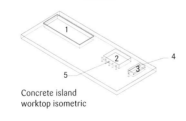

Concrete island worktop isometric

1. Cooktop cutout
2. Sink cutout
3. Strainer cutout
4. Concrete lip to allow for drinking plate to be inset flush with worktop
5. Tap holes shown indicatively

Detailed island plan

(See taps key)

0   75 cm

1. 115 cm Barazza LAB 1PLB3TI flush and built-in cooktop
2. Decorative concrete works
3. 510 x 405 Dornbracht 38050000 undermounted sink water unit
4. 210 x 405 Dornbracht 38001000 undermounted strainer water unit
5. Drinking plate (removable) Dornbracht, 84710000
6. Sink
7. Strainer

A: Dornbracht 1785168o hot and cold water dispenser
B: Dornbracht 82437970 integrated washing-up liquid dispenser
C: Dornbracht 10714970 air switch (control button) for controlling waste disposal
D, E: Dornbracht 3280068o two-hole mixer with individual rosettes
F: Dornbracht27714970 rinsing spray set

Kitchen island

082

Dark, muted colors can really set a sophisticated tone in home décor. They make a space look cozy yet elegant. They also add depth, especially when they serve as backdrops to lighter-color items. Shiny objects in particular sparkle with the right lighting.

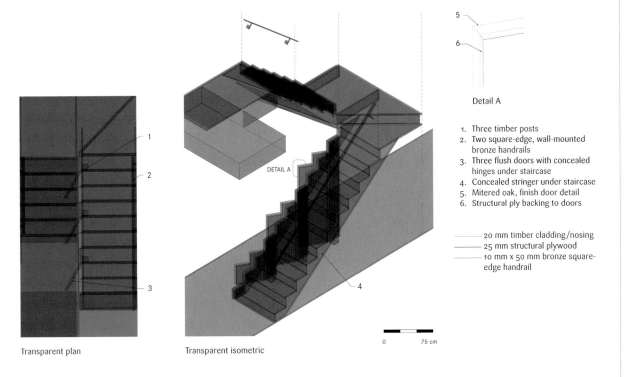

Detail A

1. Three timber posts
2. Two square-edge, wall-mounted bronze handrails
3. Three flush doors with concealed hinges under staircase
4. Concealed stringer under staircase
5. Mitered oak, finish door detail
6. Structural ply backing to doors

——— 20 mm timber cladding/nosing
——— 25 mm structural plywood
——— 10 mm x 50 mm bronze square-edge handrail

Transparent plan

Transparent isometric

0   75 cm

Proposed ground to second floor staircase

While the new design maintains the original architectural features of the building, new elements are conceived so as not to compete for attention. Nonetheless, these new elements, like the staircase, don't lack in eye-catching detail.

083

Even spaces like dressing
or powder rooms can make
design statements. Turn them
into rooms where you would
like to spend time. Use your
favorite colors, and fill these
spaces with some of your
most cherished items.

The Maryland is a nicely aged one-hundred-year-old condo building. It used to house wealthy miners while they waited for their real mansions to be built. Decades later, a meticulous restoration and upgrade of one of its apartments brings back to life the splendor of its origins with newly stained floors, fresh wallpaper, a renovated kitchen and bathroom, and good lighting. The color palette is a blend of muted colors, balanced nicely by the abundant natural light. The result is a contemporary home with clever nods to the past.

The Maryland

**cityhomeCOLLECTIVE
Cody Derrick, owner/designer**

Salt Lake City, Utah,
United States

© Lucy Call

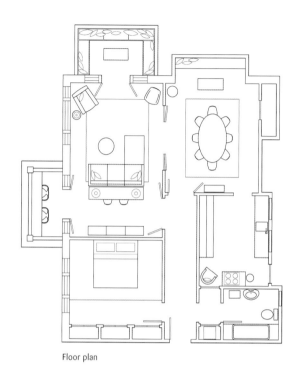

Floor plan

The one-bedroom, one-bath apartment
is filled with history. Yet it complies with
the standards of contemporary living.

084

The smallest room of the apartment is actually the most space efficient, filled with design solutions to make the most of minimal space. For instance, the custom-built benches are hollowed out for storage.

The design concept was guided by the desire to maintain the authenticity of the apartment. To achieve this goal, the original woodwork was restored to preserve the authenticity of the spaces.

The kitchen is only a hundred square feet and keeps an old charm. The priority during the design process was not to turn the kitchen into a modern cookery. As with all the other rooms in the apartment, the goal was to maintain the character of the original building.

The bedroom is an undeviating sample of single hues. It's stark, even without comparison to the rest of the home. A single paint color covers all but the floor. The huge bed sits on a custom-built platform, marked only by dim perimeter lighting. Two dry-erase boards with old sketches by the owner's tattoo-artist friend hover over the bed.

Madison Avenue Duplex

D'Aquino Monaco

Manhattan, New York,
United States

© Joshua McHugh

This duplex penthouse was remodeled around the owner's desire to display a significant art collection in a contemporary setting. The design makes the most of an original plan with few structural elements. This allowed for the creation of an apartment with an open feel that promotes a fluid circulation between areas. The clean lines of the furniture and the absence of ornament let the artwork take center stage. A neutral color palette brings in a few splashes of color only to reinforce the presence of the vibrant art pieces.

The first floor was designed around an
open plan to promote a space suitable
for entertaining. In contrast, the master
suite, with a terrace lining two of its
sides, provides for a private, quiet zone.

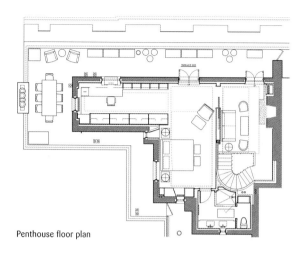

Penthouse floor plan

Ninth floor plan

A Tab coffee table from **M2L** and vintage club chairs from **Van Den Akker** on a custom rug by D'Aquino Monaco add a retro style to the living room.

085

The placement of artwork in a room is important, but so is the selection and arrangement of furniture around the artwork. The art pieces will have a greater impact when they share the space with furniture that supports them through color and form.

The open kitchen abuts the dining area, where **Poltrona Frau**'s H_T table is surrounded by chairs from **Promemoria** and **Fritz Hansen** and lit by a 1960s chandelier from **Kerson**.

The design team's greatest intervention was moving the staircase to create a gracious entrance and subsequently an upstairs sitting room.

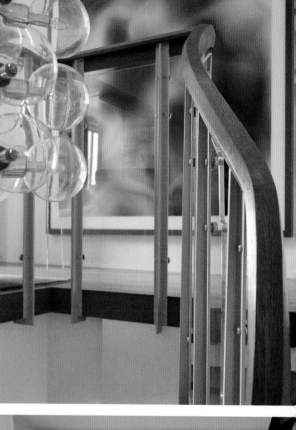

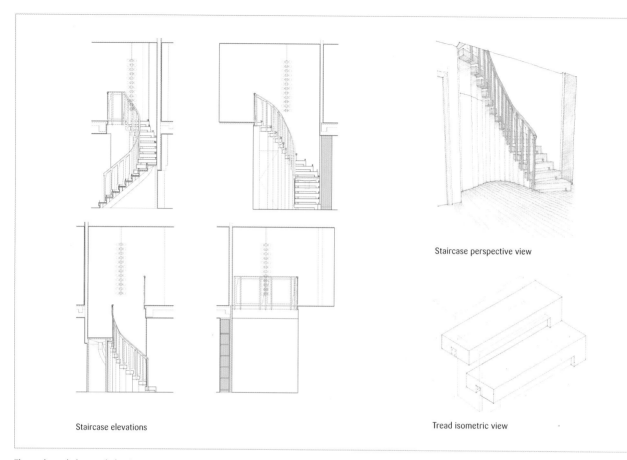

Staircase elevations

Staircase perspective view

Tread isometric view

The sculptural glass-and-aluminum staircase is a central element of the apartment's design. Its curvy yet strong lines join forces with some key furniture—such as the Vladimir Kagan's classic Serpentine sofa for **Ralph Pucci** in the living area—to soften the linearity of the apartment's structure.

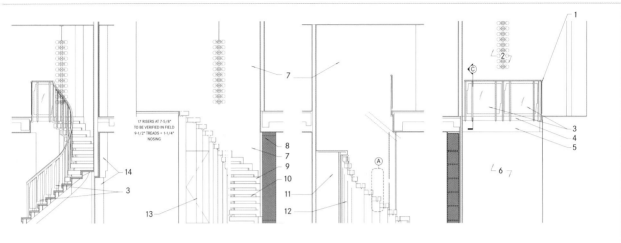

17 RISERS AT 7-5/8"
TO BE VERIFIED IN FIELD
9-1/2" TREADS • 1-1/4"
NOSING

Staircase elevations

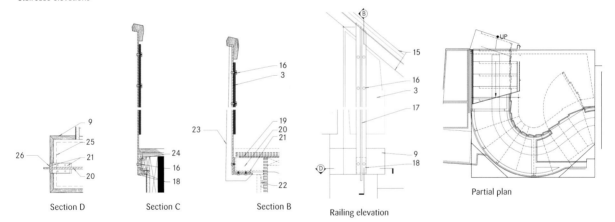

Section D   Section C   Section B   Railing elevation   Partial plan

Staircase and railing details

1. Wood handrail with tee-section steel balusters
2. Open to sitting room
3. Starphire glass panels with polished edges
4. Wood fascia stained to match wood flooring
5. Gypboard fascia, painted
6. Open to foyer
7. Venetian plaster finish
8. Lacquer cabinetry
9. Oak tread and nosing stained to match floor
10. Lacquered millwork riser
11. Steel structure
12. Stepped gypboard wall with venetian plaster finish
13. Lacquered millwork door with overlapping panels
14. Polished plaster finish
15. Wood handrail, finished to match treads
16. Fastener, to be determined, painted to match baluster
17. Tee-section baluster, painted steel; color and finish to be determined
18. Flanges of tee flush with face of tread side and bottom
19. Steel-tread support plate
20. Vertical fin plate
21. Angle bracket welded to fin plate for attachment of baluster
22. Wall and tread finishes shown dashed
23. Web of tee section tapers toward top of baluster
24. Angle bracket on blocking for attachment of balusters
25. Steel-tread support plate shown dashed
26. Tee-section baluster bolted to angle bracket

086

The color scheme is dominated by neutral colors to achieve a calm atmosphere, while a classic Saarinen Womb chair adds visual punch. The same design strategy is carried out in the office, where the orange leather chair is the focal point of the room.

087

Texture makes up for the lack of color in the bathrooms. Heavily patterned marble brings visual interest, and wood adds warmth.

Urban Vibrancy

Art Buro
Paris, France
© Art Buro

The apartment is full of contemporary urban accents and perfectly combines the influences of two vibrant cities: Paris and London. Art Buro, together with a cabinetry design team from London, WRKBNCH, has created a contemporary living space with a chic and elegant modern style. The herringbone wood floors and decorative wall panels are a traditional and elegant backdrop to a selection of contemporary furniture, which mixes iconic pieces from high-end designer furniture-manufacturing companies—including **Cassina**, **Minotti**, and **Vitra**—with bespoke pieces that offer a variety of storage solutions.

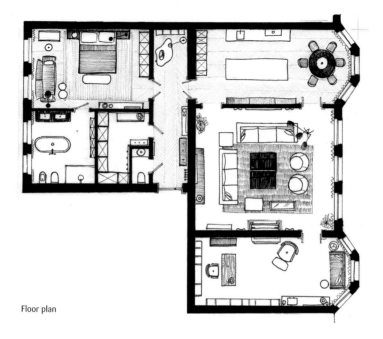

Floor plan

View A: tall units

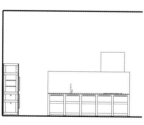

View B: units

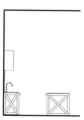

View C: units + island

View D: island

View E: island

TALL UNITS

UNITS

ISLAND

Top view

The kitchen, from WRKBNCH's K*BOX collection, is made of natural and black-painted oak and composed of drawers and pullout base units. The composition is finished off by an elegant marble worktop and wall panel.

088

BOX*C is a multifunctional cabinet in bright turquoise on a brass tubular base. It can be used as entertainment center, dressing table, or office desk.

The comfortable bed upholstered in check-patterned wool, the side tables with built-in lights, the BOX*W modular armoire in dark stained oak with black steel handles—these elements combine to give this bedroom a warm, cozy, calm feel. The armoire's interior is equipped with shelves, hanger space, a door-mounted mirror, and drawers.

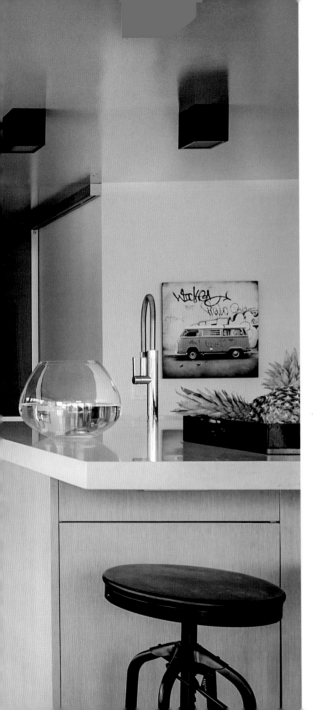

Concrete Jungle

PROjECT

Chicago, Illinois, United States
© Chris Bradley

The home's existing conditions presented a long and narrow living space that felt tight and confined. Nonetheless, the bones were there, and the space showed great potential. The design brief given by the client could be summed up in two words: colorful and fun. Working with such awkwardly proportioned space presented some challenges, but the client was fairly adventurous and willing to accept major changes. The goal was to define an open area with zones for cooking, working, and lounging, while creating a more expansive feel and improving circulation flow throughout the space.

089

The building itself, with its modern, masculine, and sleek appeal, served as inspiration for the design. Fun objects and accessories and pops of color provide the finishing touches.

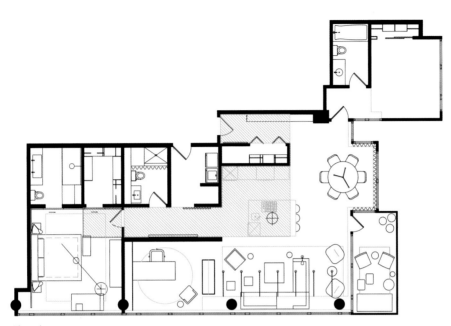

Floor plan

Walls are torn down to open up the space; a bank of cabinets extends from the entry into the living area, creating a foyer and directing circulation; and a double-sided steel-clad fireplace organizes the living area.

The bank of cabinets is clad in horizontal ebonized wood planks, accentuating the path from the entry door to the spacious living area. The dark color gives weight to the space.

Narrow passages give way to spacious areas in a dynamic play of proportion, color, and texture, giving each space a specific identity.

090

Old items can be repurposed in a creative and unusual fashion. For instance, a set of factory doors with chipped paint and rusty hardware is an eye-catching addition to a sleek bedroom décor.

Yaletown Loft

ZWADA home

Vancouver, British Columbia,
Canada

© Kyo Sada

This project presented the opportunity to explore the interior-
design possibilities for a bachelor's pad. The goal was to
create an environment that reflected a masculine sensibility.
The clean lines, subdued color palette, beautiful woods, and
varied textures found throughout the loft contribute to its
desired atmosphere, which is simultaneously luxurious and
comfortable.

The main living area, which boasts high
ceilings and large windows, features
an imposing sculptural fireplace that
anchors the room.

Floor plan

A. Entry
B. Gym
C. Living area
D. Dining area
E. Kitchen
F. Cellar

G. Bathroom
H. Laundry room
I. Den
J. Master bedroom
K. Dressing room
L. Master bathroom

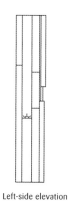

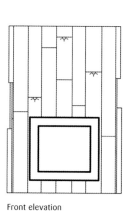

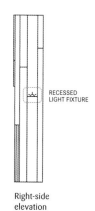

RECESSED
LIGHT FIXTURE

Left-side elevation

Front elevation

Right-side
elevation

Fireplace elevations

Gray tones, sleek leather, and pure forms were chosen for the den, in keeping with the masculine-sensibility theme.

Off the living room, an enclosed balcony offered an ideal opportunity for a gym. The two spaces, separated by Japanese shoji screens, allow light to filter into the living room, complementing the design of the windows.

An unused storage room was converted into a wine cellar, which in turn became one of the main design features of the apartment and maintained the theme of masculinity.

091

The modern bachelor's pad evokes immaculate flair, mixing form and function with rich textures and generally muted colors.

092

The sophisticated appeal of modern vanities—which feature clean, straight lines—are particularly suited for masculine bathrooms.

A.D. House

Ofist
Istanbul, Turkey
© Ali Bekman

The remodel of an apartment in a century-old residential building injects new life into the old, redundant space. The main challenge was the need to bring the space up to contemporary living standards while maintaining its historic character.
The new design embraces the existing brick walls, vaulted ceilings, gypsum decorative elements, old floor tiles, and wood paneling. Rather than recreate the aesthetics of the original space from scratch, the design team explored the possibilities that the spaces had to offer, through a creative use of readily available materials and fixtures.

Floor plan

A. Entrance   F. Dining room
B. Master bedroom   G. Bathroom
C. Guest bedroom   H. Dressing room
D. Kitchen   I. Utility room
E. Living room

The long hallway is broken in two by a
wide central area that separates the social
spaces at one end of the hallway from
the private rooms at the opposite end.

093

A fabric-covered panel has aesthetic and functional purposes: It creates a focal point in the room while, at the same time, improving its acoustics.

094

Transparent or translucent
partitions effectively separate
adjacent spaces while
maintaining an open feel and
allowing light to filter through.

095

A panel of ceramic tiles attached to an existing brick wall is a visually attractive support for open shelving. Its smooth surface is more suitable than brick for leaning furniture against.

096

A customized freestanding shower on casters and flexible hoses is completely detached from both floor and walls. This design solution enhances the distinction between container and inserted element and does not interfere with the floor and wall finishes.

097

A low shelf-headboard extends beyond the sides of the bed to serve as bedside tables. Both the shelf and a matching large frame above the bed are wedge shaped to correct the angle of the wall and make the room square.

Located on the second-to-last floor of a five-story neoclassical building, the apartment enjoys breathtaking views of the city and benefits from abundant natural light. The makeover of the apartment, which included new finishes and furnishings, respected the original features. But what really stands out about this project is the coordination that took place between the designer in Brazil, the furniture maker in Portugal, and home-décor suppliers in France. The renovation was completed with artwork purchased at the Marché aux Puces and at Galerie Maeght.

Paris Apartment

Diego Revollo
Paris, France
© Alain Brugier

098

Combine designer furniture
with custom-made joinery
for a décor that not only
integrates nicely in the
available space, but also
avoids a showroom look.

099

Mirrors can brighten a dark room and enhance the illusion of space.

The selection of furniture includes pieces by Scandinavian designer Georg Jensen and manufacturers **Roche Bobois, Minotti**, and **B&B Italia**. The light fixture by the sofa is by Serge Mouille.

100

Custom-built furniture can accurately adapt to the irregular angles of walls and make the most of the limited space available.

Floor plan

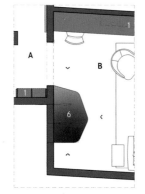

Plan view of dining table.
Open position

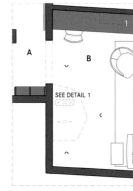

Plan view of dining table.
Closed position

A. Hall
B. Living room

1. Existing furniture
2. Existing plaster molding
3. Existing baseboard
4. Mirror-clad jambs and header
5. Wallpaper
6. High-gloss, brown lacquered dining table with glass top, color to match table or transparent
7. Mirror-clad wall

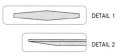

DETAIL 1

DETAIL 2

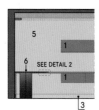
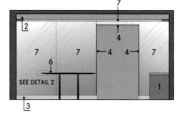

Living room partial elevations

101

Galley kitchens allow for an efficient work triangle—refrigerator, sink, and stove—when there is limited space. A good option would be to place the refrigerator and the sink on one side, and the stove on the other, between the other two.

102

The small bedroom has a wall-to-wall headboard, anchoring the room and adding weight to the bed, while the pattern of the dark-gray feature wall accentuates the horizontality of the room.

East 53rd Street
Manhattan Apartment

Eisner Design

Manhattan, New York,
United States

© Steven Mays

A three-bedroom apartment was created by uniting two smaller
units. The owner, who has spent a great deal of his career
in Asia, wanted his new home to reflect his interest in Asian
culture. One of the main features of the apartment is a curved
wall at the entry. This wall, finished in polished plaster, is
punctuated with walnut niches for the display of Asian artifacts.
The most important of these artifacts are two historically
significant samurai swords, whose shape served as inspiration
for the design of the wall. Another key feature of the design
is a wooden canopy that defines a shrine-like space within a
larger area.

An L-shape wood canopy and corresponding L-shape bench define a small entry foyer. The design takes its cue from the curved display wall.

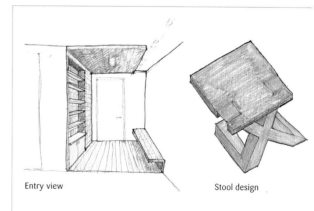

Entry view

Stool design

A fairly compact bathroom accommodates all the necessary fixtures, including a two-sink vanity, toilet, curbless shower, soaking tub, and storage. The curbless shower and freestanding tub amplify the room.

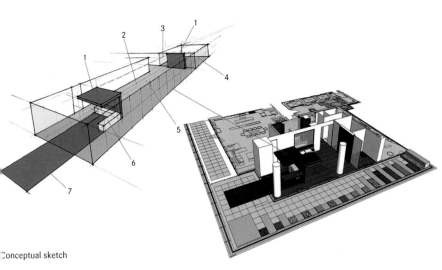

Conceptual sketch

1. Wood type 1: extends to outdoor space
2. Wood type 2: main floor
3. Translucent sliding glass doors
4. Changing area
5. Sleeping area
6. Working area
7. Outdoor

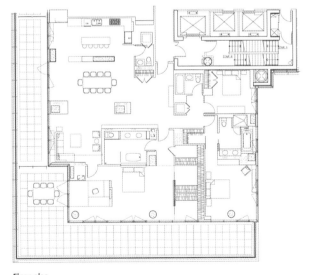

Floor plan

The stone-clad fireplace is one focal point in the grand living area, another one being a tall table extending from the wall between the kitchen and the dining area. These focal points organize the space and provide each area with its own identity.

103

Open walls between the kitchen and an adjoining room, such as a living, dining, or family room, create the perception of increased space, establishing visual connections that expand beyond the kitchen walls.

104

A counter-height table can
provide for informal meals.
From a layout standpoint,
it can serve to separate the
kitchen from the living and
dining area in open-plan
homes.

The master bedroom has a central divider-canopy wood piece similar to the one at the entry. It serves as headboard on one side and defines a study area on the other.

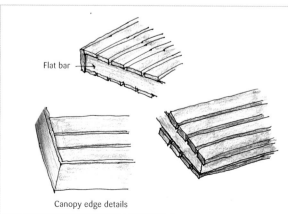

Flat bar

Canopy edge details

The flooring pattern on the study side echoes the slatted construction of the divider-canopy piece. This design detail clearly demarcates the area.

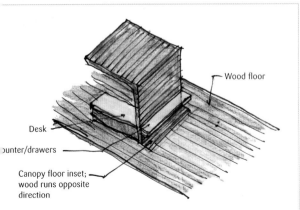

Wood floor

Desk

Counter/drawers

Canopy floor inset; wood runs opposite direction

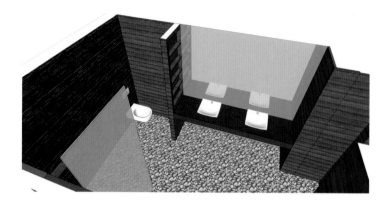

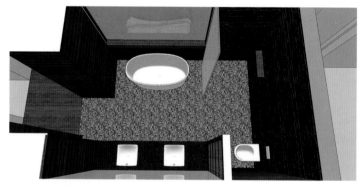

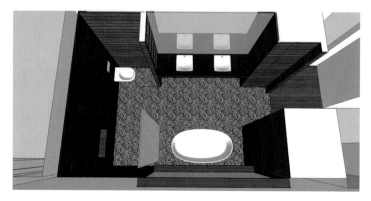

Three-dimensional views of bathroom

105

Advances in technology allow manufacturers to produce moisture-resistant materials that can provide a bathroom with elegant, warm touches. Wood has made its way into bathrooms, cladding surfaces from floor to ceiling.

106

Choose furniture for your kids' rooms that makes them want to spend time in the space. Playful furniture can have the same effect as toys: they both fill children's rooms with positive energy.

107

The blue, green, and pale-oxide tones of the tiles give the bathroom an aqueous appearance, which creates a relaxing, spa-like atmosphere.

Fifth Avenue Modern

Jessica Gersten Interiors

Manhattan, New York,
United States

© Lucia Engstrom

Mid-century classics mix with contemporary furnishings in this Fifth Avenue apartment overlooking New York City's Central Park and Guggenheim Museum. Straight lines and blocky shapes contrast with slender forms. Earthy and spicy tones and organic patterns and textures add visual interest and create a warm and inviting atmosphere. These elements come together to create unique spaces that express the sophisticated taste of the owner.

108

Wallpapers offer a wide range of designs to suit all tastes and budgets. From geometric to floral, explore the endless possibilities with bold patterns to create a feature wall, or with subtle prints to cover all the walls of a room. It's all about finding the ideal balance.

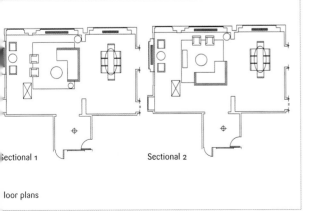

Sectional 1   Sectional 2

loor plans

109

What we see through our windows is almost as important as the design of an interior space. Like colors used in a room, views can affect our mood. Looking at another building a few feet away is nothing like looking at natural scenes.

A large piece of wall art enlivens this dining room with warm and bright colors, harmonizing with the wood dining table and chairs. Also, the format of the artwork echoes the proportions of the doorway leading to the kitchen.

The designs of the children's rooms have a soft yet modern and fun approach. Light tones with playful details add warmth and color.

110

A feature wall at the head of the bed can provide an instant draw and can express an unspoken invitation to get comfortable and intimate.

La Jolla Beach Cottage

CM Natural Designs

La Jolla, California,
United States

© Chipper Hatter

This charming interior embraces the simplicity of the beach
cottage style with an eclectic mix of rustic and modern
furnishings and crisp, cool tones that contrast with splashes
of vibrant colors, warm textures, and nautical accents. The
designer has successfully captured the spirit of living by the
sea, and did so without displaying shells and driftwood, but
instead more abstract designs. Beyond the clear connections
to the sea and sand dunes, the design offers comfortable
year-round living.

111

Mix rustic and contemporary furniture in a room to achieve casual elegance. Pattern and texture add visual and tactile interest.

Living and dining area's materials and furnishings mood boards

112

Rustic and contemporary pieces of furniture are skillfully mixed in a room of contrasting features: hard and soft, square and round, boxlike and slender.

Living and dining area plan

In keeping with the style of the home, the breakfast nook is an inviting area of contrasting colors. The wood tabletop and the woven lampshade add warmth.

113

White beadboard cabinet fronts give a kitchen the clean, lived-in, inviting look that the cottage style affords.

Den's materials and furnishings mood board

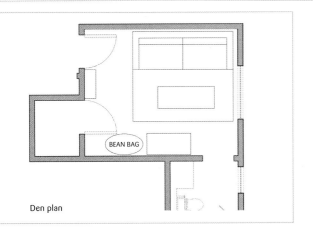

BEAN BAG

Den plan

The dark-gray wall and cerulean-blue area rug provide the room with depth, while the bright-red couch adds energy. The setting is completed with a wood coffee table and picture frames, and the patterned throw pillows and blanket add visual interest.

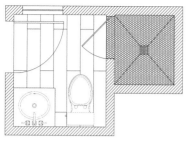

Den bathroom plan

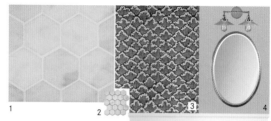

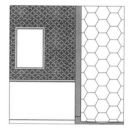

1   2   3   4

1. 10" hexagon-honed Calcutta shower wall tile
2. 1" hexagon-honed Calcutt shower floor tile
3. Wallpaper above molding
4. Light-gray paint behind mirror
5. Porcelain plank flooring
6. White paint below moldin

5   6

Den bathroom's materials and finishes mood board

North elevation

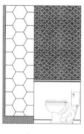

West elevation

East elevation

South elevation

Den bathroom elevations

The white wainscot anchors the plumbing fixtures and the vanity, all in the same color. The wallpaper and paint color above the wainscot, paired with the wavy pattern of the white marble tile, follows the nautical theme.

Guest bedroom's materials and furnishings mood board

The sea-inspired color scheme gives
the room a comfortable and fresh look,
accented by high-contrast elements,
such as a black headboard, drawer
chest, and mirror frame.

Guest bedroom plan

Master bedroom's materials and furnishings mood board

Master bedroom plan

1. Shower walls and water-closet tile
2. Shower-feature wall tile
3. Shower floor tile
4. Color elevation feature wall at shower
5. Vanity lighting
6. Existing vanity and countertop
7. Porcelain wood-plank flooring

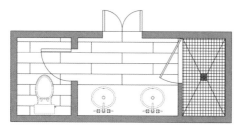

Master bathroom material and furnishings mood board

Master bathroom plan

Master bathroom elevations

114

Consider limiting your
bathroom color scheme to
two colors or to one main
color combined with two
accent colors. The decision
may depend on the size of the
bathroom and the complexity
of its layout.

115

The complexity of your bathroom-tile design will depend on budget, but possibilities are endless, whether you cover all surfaces using a single type of tile, or create more complex designs.

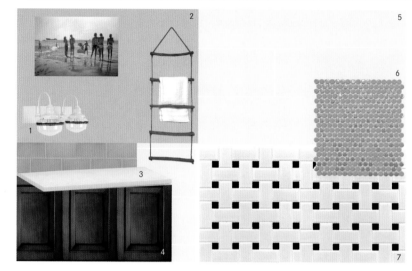

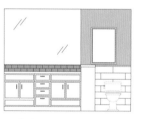

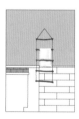

Guest bathroom materials and furnishings mood board

1. Vanity lighting
2. Gray paint on all walls
3. Glass backsplash tile
4. Existing vanity with new quartz countertop
5. White plank shower wall and bathroom wall tile
6. Sea-foam penny shower floor tile
7. Basket-weave floor tile

South elevation

West elevation

North elevation

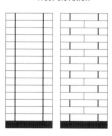

Two tile detail options for the shower walls

Guest bathroom elevations

116

Small statement tiles generally serve better as features in a bathroom, rather than its main attraction. They can also be made to match other features of the room, such as cabinets and plumbing fixtures.

Guest bathroom plan

When the owner decided to make this cottage his home, he sought out Kelly Mittleman of Kelly and Co. Design. He had seen her design work and liked the way she mixed modern and traditional in a modern farmhouse style. The design approach was aimed at adapting the original structure to a more contemporary use and expanding the sense of space without modifying its footprint. As a result, the house, which is only 2,100 square feet, fulfills all the functions of a contemporary dwelling. At the same time, its raised ceilings and large openings make it feel spacious and bright.

Modern Farmhouse Cottage

Kelly and Co. Design

Easton, Connecticut, United States

© Jane Beiles

The entire cottage was gutted, but the original pine paneling and river-stone fireplace were maintained. Kelly and Co. Design added batten-and-board trim work and vaulted all the ceilings, trimming them in shiplap to add character.

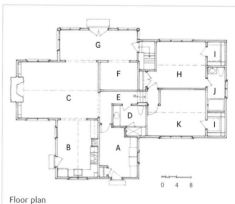

Floor plan

A. Mud room / laundry roo[m]
B. Kitchen
C. Living / dining room
D. Bathroom
E. Hall
F. Den
G. Sunroom
H. Master bedroom
I. Walk-in clos[et]
J. Master bathroom
K. Bedroom

0 4 8

The kitchen was designed to keep the farmhouse feel with hutches and cupboards, while the wide-sawn white-oak floor brings in a subtle contemporary touch. The olive-green color of the cabinets rounds off the design, introducing a touch of nature.

117

Crisp, white interiors evoke
modernity, coolness, and
serenity. In this case, these
mostly white interiors with
accents of earthy tones and
soft textiles capture the spirit
of casual cottage life.

118

Contrast in texture adds
interest to a room with a
color palette of similar tones.
At a different level, light can
accentuate color and textural
variations, producing a soft
and inviting atmosphere.

The master bath gives a nod to the exotic with its Moroccan tiled floor, but it maintains the shiplap on the walls as a recurring leitmotif of the design.

119

Steel-framed shower enclosures with divided glass panes generally offer an industrial look, but they are compatible with a more rustic aesthetic when other elements—such as mirrors, plumbing, and light fixtures—help integrate them into the décor.

Loft Great Jones

Union Studio

Manhattan, New York,
United States

© Mathew Bear, Rosie Trenholm

Black-and-white finishes mix with the brick and steel of an original industrial space converted into a home. An ample space accommodating a living and dining area and an open kitchen conveniently separates two private zones at opposite ends of the long and narrow loft. Thus the proportions of the different zones appear less elongated and therefore better adapted to a comfortable living environment.

Heirloom-quality furniture is the signature of the design company, whose philosophy is driven by the particular expression of materials.

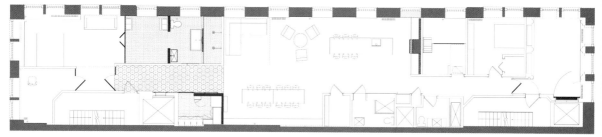

Floor plan

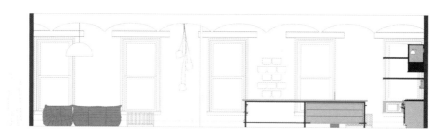

Living room / kitchen north elevation

Kitchen east elevation

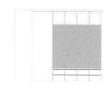

Laundry room
south elevation

Laundry room
east elevation

Laundry room
north elevation

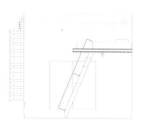

Child's bedroom east
elevation

Child's bedroom south
elevation

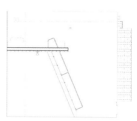

Child's bedroom west
elevation

The west end of the loft includes a small office and the master bedroom with en suite bathroom. The east end has two bedrooms and a larger office. The central space, which accomodates all the daytime activities, is sparsely furnished with bespoke and designer pieces to maintain an airy feel.

The fully equipped kitchen boasts a
bespoke white-oak and black-steel
island, as well as a custom hood and
pot rack, a **Wolf** range, a **Sub-Zero**
refrigerator, stools from **Fyrn,** and island
lighting from **Olde Good Things**.

© Union Studio

Kitchen island perspective rendering

120

Using one single dark color
in a room creates a sense
of continuity and serenity
because there are no color
contrasts to draw the eye.

121

Vintage furniture, metal light fixtures, and metallic surfaces celebrate a style that exposes original, raw elements and finishes as a reminder of the industrial past of a space.

122

Steel-framed glass partitions
and doors have become a
popular design solution to
impart an industrial look,
while at the same time
providing a space with a
sense of openness.

A custom-made headboard of salvaged white oak leans against a wall of black tiles designed by Marcel Wanders for **Bisazza**. Union Studio designed the steel-framed partitions and doors with pebbled wire glass.

Shelves and dresser designed by Matthew Bear/Union Stud

Shelves and dresser are
custom made in black steel
and teak. Still in line with the
industrial look of the loft, they
add warmth and a homey
touch.

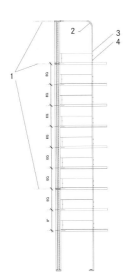

Front elevation

Side elevation

Front elevation

Side elevation

1. Centerline of window system horizontal
2. 2" interior radius
3. 3/8" x 1" flat bar
4. #8 1 ¼" round head slotted steel wood screw
5. #10 machine screw
6. #10 machine screw; upright on closet entry system predrilled and tapped for backsplash screws
7. #10 machine screws; top horizontal on closet entry system predrilled and tapped or top attachment
8. #8 1 ¼" round head slotted steel wood screw

1. 3/8" x 1" HRS flat bar
2. #8 round head slotted wood screw
3. 2" interior radius
4. #10 machine screw
5. Teak outer case
6. Plywood inner case

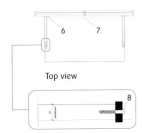

Top view

Section through vertical standard at backsplash

Teak shelves west

Top view

Teak shelves east

Teak shelves east perspective rendering

Teak shelves west perspective rendering

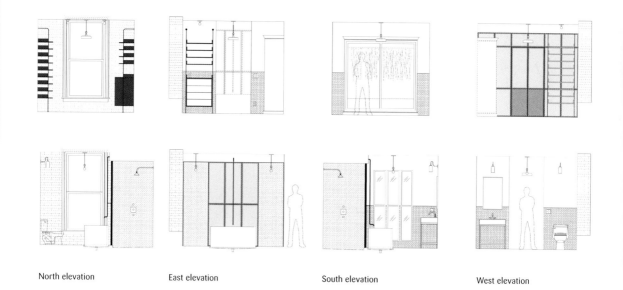

North elevation

East elevation

South elevation

West elevation

Master bathroom

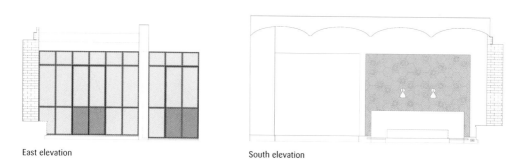

East elevation

South elevation

Master bedroom

A custom teak soaking tub and spout take center stage in the master bathroom. The floor tiles are 12-inch hexagonal concrete Andy Fleishman tiles through **Anne Sacks**. Wainscoting is clipped black marble mosaic through **Waterworks**, and the shower wall tile is white marble "Facet" tile through **Walker Zanger**.

Loft Lovell

Union Studio

Mill Valley, California,
United States

© Matthew Bear, Ilana Diamond

Originally built as a library around 1910 and used as such until
1966, the brick and timber two-story building fell into disrepair
and changed hands a few times as a private residence. None of
the original interior was intact by the time the current owners
purchased it, except for an original bookcase that was kept
in the living room to house an extensive periodical collection.
The building had to be seismically reinforced. This offered
the opportunity to take the interior down to its bare structure
and create a blank canvas on which the new interior could be
developed.

The focus was on creating an open, family-oriented space for the new owners, both of whom work in design and are parents of two young children. The goal was to facilitate creativity at all levels.

Upper floor plan

Lower floor plan

The material palette for the entire home emphasizes solid natural beauty, durability, and ease of maintenance. The entry foyer is floored in black marble slabs in contrast with the rest of the floors, which are solid, wide-plank white oak with a light-gray wash and matte finish. Blackened hot-rolled steel is used as a panel material throughout.

Union Studio designed all the specialty custom steel work. The cabinetry and built-ins throughout the entire residence were created from solid American black walnut.

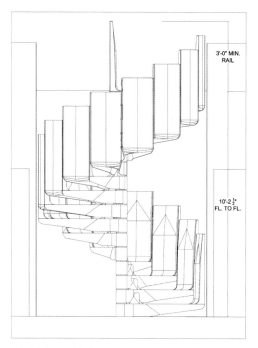

3'-0" MIN.
RAIL

10'-2 ½"
FL. TO FL.

Spiral staircase elevation

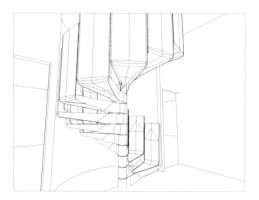

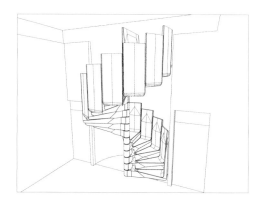

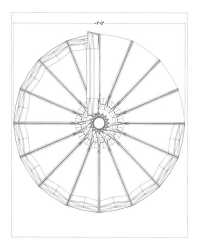

~7'-0"

Spiral staircase plan

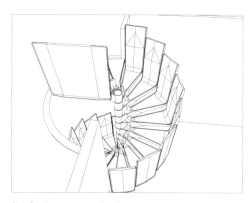

Spiral staircase perspective views

...aircase designed in collaboration with Geza Gergo

123

Black hot-rolled steel develops a pattern when exposed to moisture in the atmosphere, which gives the metal a unique look. Its smooth texture invites touch and reflects light in muted tones.

The dining space occupies a corner dominated by recessed shelves installed in what were formerly windows. The windows had been removed and a box was constructed behind the openings during a previous remodel when a newer building was constructed a few feet from the back wall.

Situated on the second floor in a space that connects a large living room and studio, the kitchen is flanked on one side by the service staircase and a block of cabinetry. The island—under a new three-by-sixteen-foot skylight—responds to the clients' desire for a communal cooking experience.

The project enhances the architectural
features of the preexisting building.
Soft, earth-toned furnishings harmonize
with the warm tones of the oak floor
and brick walls.

124

Inspired by the artful work of American furniture maker George Nakashima, the design of these dining tables with unfinished edges highlights the expressive power of natural wood.

125

Various skylights were installed to compensate for the lack of natural light on the second floor. In both the master bathroom and the kitchen, the skylights reflect the proportions of what is below them: the kitchen island and the bathroom vanity area.

126

A Charles Eames chaise longue—originally created for a Museum of Modern Art competition in 1948—adds a touch of artistic finesse with its white, organic form, contrasting with the roughness and earthy tones of the brick walls.

Duplex Penthouse
Apartment

Toledano + Architects

Tel Aviv, Israel

© Oded Smadar

This duplex penthouse apartment was completely renovated to accommodate the needs of a couple with children. The floor plan provides separate areas for the members of the family, as well as spacious and modular living areas that can be adapted to suit different situations. The design emphasizes the materiality of the spaces, through a cohesive use of wood, concrete, and black metal, complemented by the powerful Middle Eastern light.

Sixth floor plan

A.	Lobby	I.	Bathroom
B.	Entry hall	J.	Washer/dryer
C.	Walk-in closet	K.	Powder room
D.	Toilet	L.	Pantry
E.	Master bedroom	M.	Kitchen
F.	Master bathroom	N.	Dining area
G.	Living room	O.	Living area
H.	Kid's bedroom	P.	Outdoor kitchen

1.	Storage	21.	Induction stove
2.	Coat closet	22.	Sink-meat
3.	Bench	23.	Sink-milk
4.	Shelves	24.	Fridge-meat
5.	Bar	25.	Fridge-milk
6.	Bookcase	26.	Wine cellar
7.	Wood door	27.	Storage
8.	Hanging rail system	28.	Table extension
9.	Cabinet	29.	Folding black metal
10.	Wood shelves on		table
	doors	30.	Dishwasher
11.	Sliding wood door	31.	Oven
12.	Wood panel	32.	Bar/worktop, black
13.	Wood platform		Caesarstone
14.	Electric meter	33.	Walnut wood
15.	4 drawers		bench
16.	Cabinet shelves	34.	Wood pergola
17.	Cabinet shelves +	35.	Wood bench
	hanger	36.	Worktop with
18.	Dryer		storage below
19.	Washer with sink	37.	BBQ
20.	Metal shelves	38.	Sink

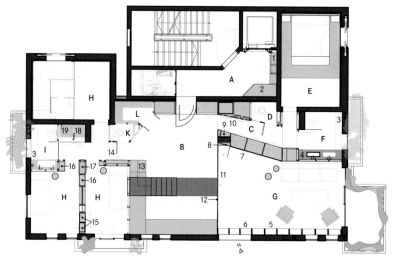

Fifth floor plan

The design of the apartment promotes a flexible use of the space through sliding panels that allow various configurations. This concept is further developed with the design of multifunctional elements, such as a hidden bar in the bookcase and an extendable folding metal table.

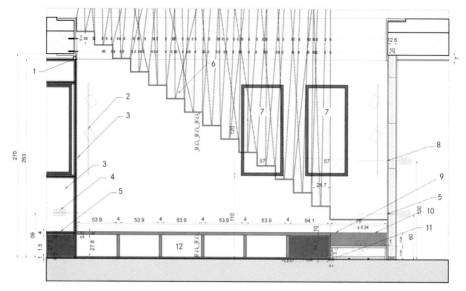

Living room bookcase, section A-A

1. Rail for doors
2. Walnut wood lamp shades mounted on black metal support
3. Walnut wood paneling
4. Two electrical outlets
5. Push-release drawer; walnut wood inside and outside
6. Wall painted white
7. Black aluminum-framed window
8. One light switch + two electrical shade switches
9. Walnut wood platform
10. Antislip surface
11. Hollow metal joint, painted black
12. Push-release drawer; walnut wood veneer

A suspended blackened steel staircase is a prominent feature of the design that adds to the apartment's creative character. The suspension rods double as guardrail forming a dense crisscross pattern.

The design of the lights above the kitchen island is a take on the steel rods suspending the staircase from the ceiling.

The suspension rods form a crisscross pattern that is projected on to the floor, creating continuously changing shadow patterns that visually enrich the space.

127

A current trend is to take the TV away from the living room or the bedroom and put it in a separate room. You can turn a spare room into a cozy TV room that can double as a home office.

Concrete can develop natural irregularities and patinas that add to the character of a space. Stained, colored, smooth, or rough—concrete surfaces boast a one-of-a-kind look, guaranteeing major design impact.

Kids' bedrooms can be planned as playful environments that promote creativity. Materials and colors are design tools that offer children a space of their own, where they can develop their own identities.

East Coast

Obllique

Singapore City, Singapore
© Bryan Van Der Beek

The extensive remodel of a 1,033-square-foot walk-up apartment from the 1960s features a contemporary interior. Two bedrooms were demolished to create an airy home for a single woman with pets. With raw-concrete and pale-wood finishes as a backdrop, the owner's eclectic collection of vintage items takes center stage. The apartment integrates various forms of built-ins to provide abundant storage space, which frees the area from additional freestanding furniture that may interfere with the easy flow of circulation.

The once overly fragmented apartment is transformed into an open space, where furniture demarcates the different functions.

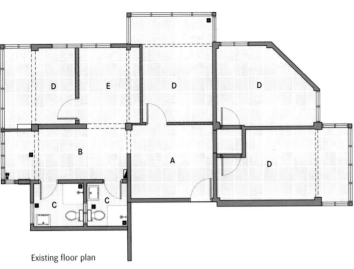

Existing floor plan

A. Foyer
B. Kitchen
C. Bathroom
D. Room
E. Living room

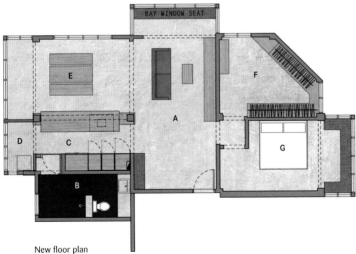

BAY WINDOW SEAT

New floor plan

A. Living area
B. Bathroom
C. Kitchen
D. Yard
E. Dining area
F. Dressing room
G. Bedroom

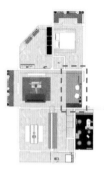

Living area perspective view: main door, shoe cabinet, and pegboard wall

130

Pegboard walls allow for changeable arrangements of shelves and hooks—a more creative alternative to prefabricated cabinets with adjustable shelving.

The design of the apartment clearly distinguishes between the existing concrete shell and the new wood elements, such as the floor-to-ceiling pegboard panels, sliding doors, window benches with storage, and kitchen equipment.

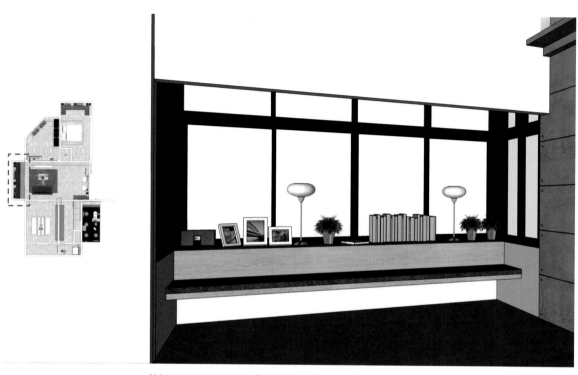

Living area perspective view: bay window seat

131

Window benches in the living room and the bedroom provide additional seating and shelving. The underside of the benches can be used for a neat arrangement of boxes, which can be in different materials and colors for a fun touch.

The kitchen is fully equipped with modern appliances integrated in a wall unit and island, which provide plenty of storage space.

Kitchen cabinet wall elevation

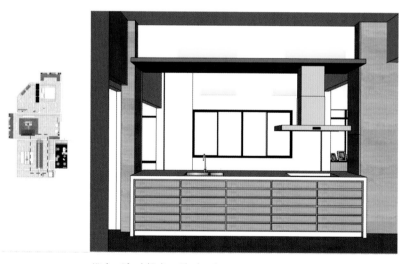

Kitchen island: kitchen side elevation

All the elements of the kitchen are clad in wood to match the woodwork used throughout. This creates a sense of unity and order within the open plan of the apartment.

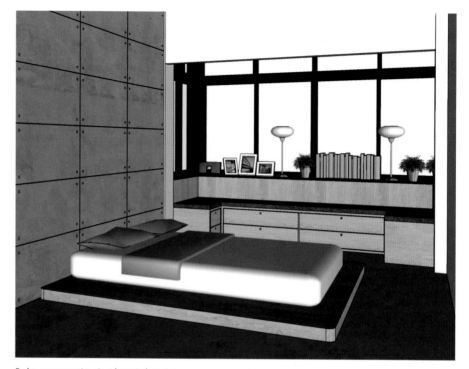

Bedroom perspective view: bay window seat

The design of the bench below the window is a variation of the one in the living room. While the underside of the bench in the living room is open, the bench in the bedroom has drawers.

The platform bed and window bench draw the eye to the low part of the bedroom, making a clear distinction between the newly installed elements and the existing structure.

You can go for the neatly organized modular system of single and double hangers, stacks of shelves and drawers, and shoe cubbies, or, for the do-it-yourself type of look, try assembling basic construction materials.

Wardrobe and storage shelf perspective view

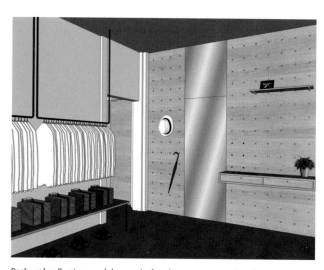

Pegboard wall, mirror, and drawers in dressing room perspective view

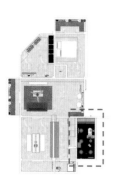

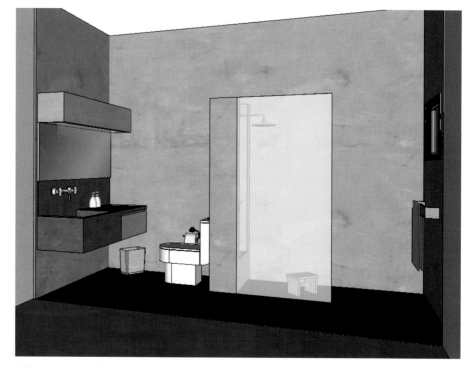

Toilet perspective view: light box, drawers, towel hanger, and door

133

The use of concrete is extended into the bathroom from the sink to the shower wall for a cohesive environment throughout.

134

Concrete is a popular material in modern bathroom design. Some bathrooms have concrete details; others are completely made of concrete, from shower floor to vanity.

Interior Villa

Beef Architekti

Průhonice, Czech Republic

© Jakub Dvořák

The new design highlights the potential of a lavish villa's generous proportions and high ceilings. The extensive remodel was carried out in two steps: first, opening up the space to achieve an airy feel and to better appreciate the existing structure; second, arranging strategically positioned volumes to allow for the separation of the different functions of the house without interfering with the fluid circulation throughout the space.

The organization of the space is achieved by means of two newly installed volumes: one is a sandstone-clad structure incorporating a fireplace; the other is a wood bookcase that partially screens off a TV room.

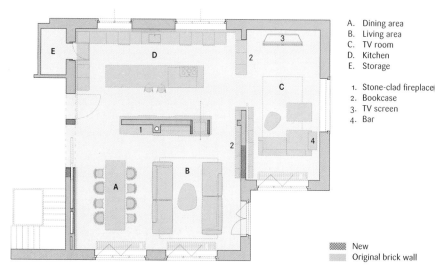

A. Dining area
B. Living area
C. TV room
D. Kitchen
E. Storage

1. Stone-clad fireplace
2. Bookcase
3. TV screen
4. Bar

New
Original brick wall

Floor plan

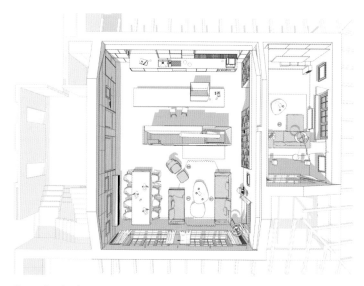

Perspective view from top

Furniture and lighting come from British, Italian, Spanish, and German manufacturers. They combine with custom-made pieces of cabinetry, such as the floating sideboard in the dining area.

The interior is in soft, natural hues of imbued black walnut, solid oak, and stone. The floor is custom-made from solid-oak planks of different sizes.

135

Spatial alignments of
partitions or furniture can
guide circulation throughout
a space, while contributing to
an orderly and harmonious
layout.

View of kitchen wall unit and island. Computer generated rendering

Optimizing the space for storage was key in the design of the apartment. The kitchen features tall cabinets against the walls between windows. The integrated tilting cutting board, knife block, and racks for spices, cutlery, and dishes make the cabinets highly functional and very stylish.

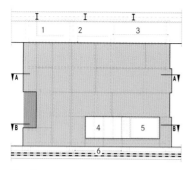

Elevation 1

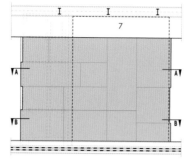

Elevation 2

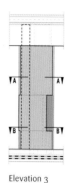

Elevation 3

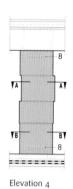

Elevation 4

1. IPN 180 beam
2. 50 mm x 50 mm Z-clip
3. 100 mm x 50 mm metal profile
4. Firewood storage
5. Rüegg Axinit Front fireplace
6. Cut holes for anchoring
7. Existing wall
8. Ventilation cutouts
9. Jakel
10. Air gap
11. Internal flashing
12. Flue
13. Existing wall, matte black paint finish
14. Anchoring foot
15. Structure

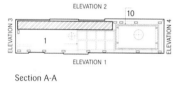

Section A-A

Section B-B

Fireplace details

The volume is clad in sandstone slabs arranged to form geometric patterns. Its strong sculptural appeal is enhanced by the different thicknesses of the stone slabs.

136

An orthogonal interior layout creates a sense of order. This effect can be further enhanced when the alignment of partitions or furniture creates a feeling of continuity and serenity.

The large bookcase is double sided, providing a generous amount of storage space. It is completely see-through in one section, allowing visual connection between the TV room and the kitchen, and it is opaque where it wraps around a wall.

Penthouse V

Beef Architekti

Bratislava, Slovakia

© Jakub Dvořák

The configuration of an existing five-room penthouse presented an inefficient floor plan. The remodel involved the removal of nonbearing walls, creating a much brighter and spacious interior. Two oak-clad volumes, one containing an open master bathroom, and the other a fireplace and bathroom, organize the different functions. In order to provide a level of privacy, daytime and nighttime areas can be separated by means of heavy linen curtains. This design gesture allows a flexible use of the space. The airy character of the new plan is further enhanced by an improved connection between the interior and the terrace.

The penthouse has three distinct areas: a cozy living area, a rigorously designed kitchen, and a semiopen bedroom. These areas are arranged along the windows and terrace walls to make the most of the natural light.

Floor plan

Various abstract trees playfully camouflage structural columns. The nature-themed design is completed with a faceted pinewood ceiling that brings to mind a dense forest canopy.

Sofa top view

Armchair
front view

Armchair section
B-B

Sofa front view

Armchair top view

Sofa section A-A

Sofa section B-B

Sofa rear view

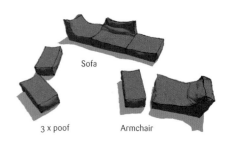

Sofa

3 x poof

Armchair

137

Linen and burlap are great
eco-friendly, natural materials
that can be used to easily
fabricate pillows and poofs
at home. These can make for
informal extra seating and add
a unique touch to a rustic,
eco-style space.

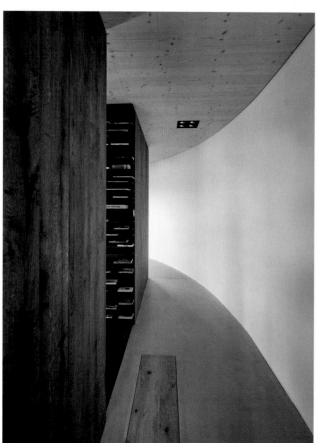

138

Different wood types, thick
fabrics for cushy seating
and heavy curtains, and a
color palette of earthy tones
come together to create a
comfortable atmosphere.

A sleek stainless steel kitchen island stands right next to a massive wood dining table and benches. The wood is left untreated to enhance the natural beauty of this material.

Three-dimensional
view of kitchen organizer

1. Refrigerator/freezer
2. Oven
3. Dishwasher

139

The kitchen's storage cabinets and appliances are concealed behind floor-to-ceiling wood pivoting pocket doors. This system offers the advantage of keeping the cabinets in an open position with no door in the way.

A separate wing of the apartment
accommodates a kid's bedroom,
providing the perfect private universe
for a child.

In keeping with the natural and rustic design aesthetic of the penthouse, the front of the bedroom's closet is made of multiple sliding doors. The slatted design camouflages the edges of the doors, achieving a seamless look.

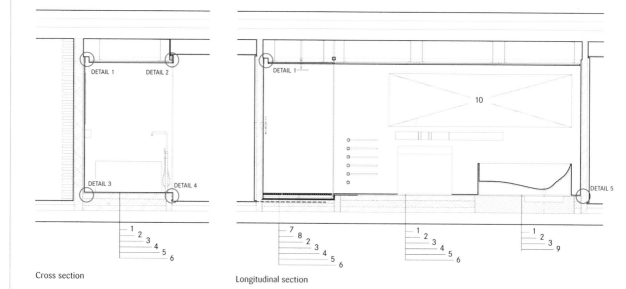

Cross section

Longitudinal section

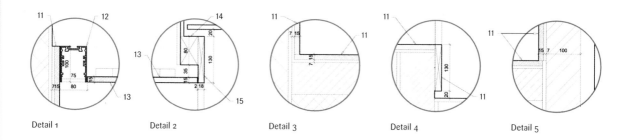

Detail 1

Detail 2

Detail 3

Detail 4

Detail 5

Master bathroom

1. Concrete flooring
2. Schomburg glue
3. Schomburg Aquafin waterproof bonding membrane
4. Concrete
5. Polystyrene
6. Self-leveling concrete layer
7. Wood shower floor
8. Concrete
9. Concrete foundation
10. Mirror
11. Concrete covering
12. Modular SL75 recessed light fixture
13. Concrete ceiling
14. Blocking
15. Wood cladding

De Korendrager

TANK Architecture & Interior Design

Amsterdam, The Netherlands

© Teo Krijgsman

TANK renovated a warehouse that had been used for a variety of uses. Originally used to store grain, the space also served as a gambling house and as an office. The design team turned this unusual place into a loftlike, fully functional residence. The new design makes the most of the the space size and enhances the existing building materials. While the remodel includes the reuse of materials found on-site, the space was radically transformed into a dwelling with modern commodities and a strong identity.

During the remodel, 150-year-old
German pine boards were discovered
under the floor material. They were
restored, and reutilized as new flooring
material in the living area and bedroom.
Similarly, the removal of dropped
ceilings exposed the old charred
beams. Together these found materials
contribute to a warm and rustic
atmosphere.

The original brick walls appeared behind stucco and layers of paint, and an anhydrite subfloor became a new finished floor, offering a concrete-like look. Glass, steel, and leather complete the material and finish scheme of the design.

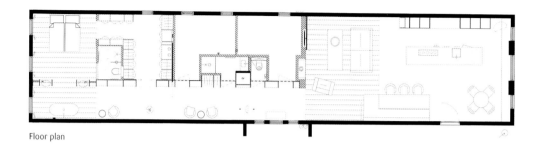

Floor plan

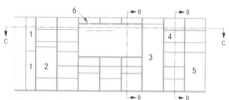

Front elevation

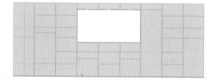

Front elevation A

Side elevation

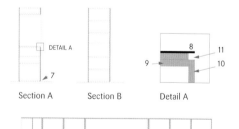

Section A   Section B   Detail A

Section C

Kitchen wall unit

1. Storage shelf
2. Dishwasher
3. Refrigerator
4. Microwave
5. Freezer
6. Spot lights mounted on shelf
7. Door's bottom edge at 18 mm above floor finish
8. Steel
9. Betonplex plywood panel
10. Door
11. Reveal around steel frame

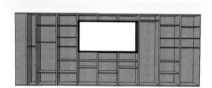

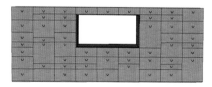

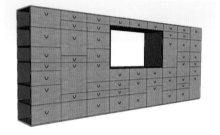

Three-dimensional views of kitchen wall unit

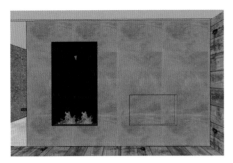

Three-dimensional view of fireplace wall

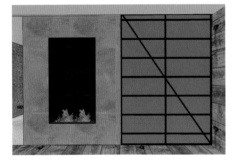

Three-dimensional view of fireplace wall with sliding door

Fireplace and TV wall

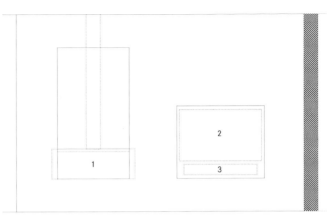

Front elevation

Plan view

1. Fireplace
2. TV
3. Speakers and bar

140

Soft colors and playful
accents come together to
give the room spirit and
individuality and to create a
space that clearly stands out
from the rest of the house
décor.

141

Kids' bedrooms seem to lend better than any other room in a home to color experimentation. They also offer opportunities for transforming ordinary items into distinctive and unique pieces.

The corridor was made deliberately wider than average to incorporate it into the living area. Along this corridor, a fifty-three-feet-long plywood bookcase frames the entrance to the bedrooms.

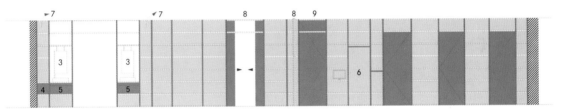

Plan

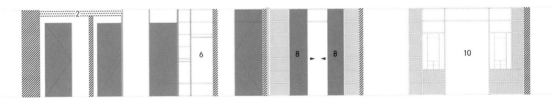

Front elevation

Section

Bookshelf

1. Double wall to accommodate electrical work
2. Area of dropped ceiling
3. Mirror
4. Valve-access trap
5. Drawer
6. Coat closet
7. Shallow shelves
8. Sliding doors
9. Ceiling-high door
10. Doorway

Detail

Three-dimensional view of
bookshelf from bedroom

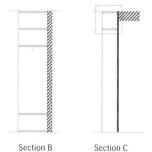

Section B   Section C

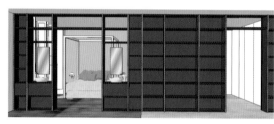

Partial three-dimensional view of bookshelf from hallway (left section)

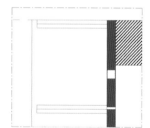

Bookshelf detail

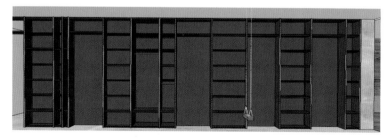

Partial three-dimensional view of bookshelf from hallway (right section)

142

The evolution in bathroom design, which mainly comes with a change in attitudes about how to utilize the space, offers a whole new world of design opportunities.

Downtown Loft

Shawn Henderson

Manhattan, New York,
United States

© Steve Freihon

The conversion of a former printing factory into a residential
loft presented an opportunity to display some pieces of the
owners' large collection of classic furniture from Wegner,
Baughman, Frankl, Poul Volther, and Dunbar, among others.
The design incorporates original architectural elements that
harmoniously coexist with new elements of contemporary
living. This was achieved by a high-quality design and exquisite
attention to detail. Various art pieces round off the design,
creating a cheerful and dynamic atmosphere.

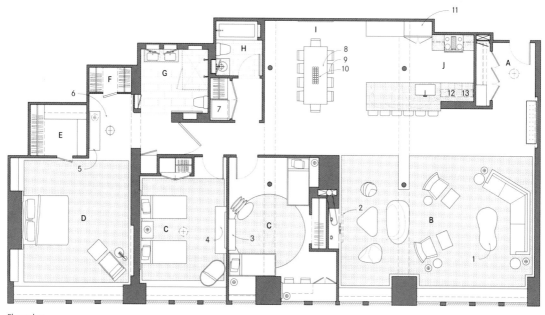

Floor plan

A. Entry
B. Living area
C. Bedroom
D. Master bedroom
E. Walk-in closet
F. Closet
G. Master bathroom
H. Bathroom
I. Dining area
J. Kitchen

1. 72"W x 36"D x 14.5"H Paul Frankl coffee table
2. TV
3. 52"W x 11.5" D x 58.5"H Wilhelm Lutjens bookshelf
4. Hans Wegner credenza
5. Milo Baughman chest of drawers
6. Tejo Remy "Accidental carpet," commissioned to size
7. Washer/dryer
8. Paul Frankl dining table
9. Tanya Aguiñiga set of Eames DCM dining chairs
10. Two Droog milk-bottle chandeliers by Tejo Remy
11. Refrigerator integrated with full height storage cabinets
12. Dishwasher
13. Wine cooler

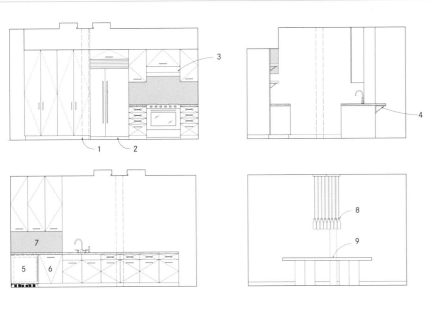

The remodel involved extensive work in the kitchen and bathrooms in order to make the loft fully functional.

Kitchen elevations

1. Line of existing column
2. Existing refrigerator to receive new door
3. Low-profile ventilation hood
4. Overhang for counter stools
5. Wine cooler
6. Dishwasher with full panel
7. Zinc backsplash
8. Two Droog milk-bottle chandeliers by Tejo Remy
9. Paul Frankl dining table

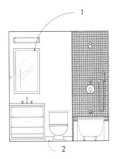
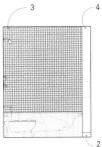
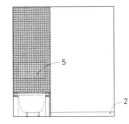
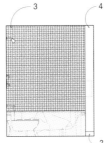

Bathroom elevations

1. Barbara Barry P73017-00-WH white medicine cabinet
2. Recessed painted wood base; dimensions to match typical base throughout
3. Glass tile
4. Sheetrock
5. Shower niche

143

Wood beams, cast-iron
columns, and vaulted brick
ceilings are commonly
incorporated as a way to
provide a newly redesigned
contemporary space with a
sense of history.

144

Spaces are often stripped of partitions in order to create open and airy interiors, leaving columns as support for sliding panels and cabinets, which in turn serve as space organizers.

This bedroom incorporates into its design original elements of the existing building: a cast-iron column painted black to stand out from the cheerful color palette, and a wood beam to contrast with the white ceiling.

145

Reconfiguring a space during a remodel often involves tearing down walls and blocking openings, which creates the opportunity to design built-ins.

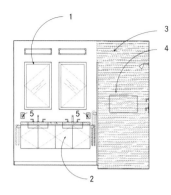

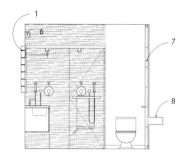

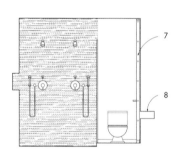

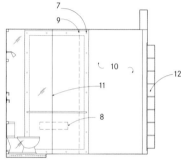

Master bathroom elevations

1. Barbara Barry P73017-00-WH white medicine cabinet
2. Wall-hung storage vanity with custom lacquered wood and stone top
3. Full-height wall tile in shower area only
4. Niche
5. New GFCI outlet
6. Sconce
7. Existing full-height sliding door
8. Niche behind sliding door for TP
9. Line of door opening beyond
10. Open to beyond
11. Line of glass partition between shower and toilet
12. Existing metal wall cabinet

146

Old buildings generally require an upgrade of the plumbing fixtures and even a redesign of drain and vent lines. If the work is substantial, chances are that little of the existing old charm will be preserved. On the bright side, this is a chance for a complete redo.

In the late 1990s, this industrial building was converted into lofts. Before that, it housed many of the notable art galleries that put Soho at the center of New York's art scene during the 1980s and 1990s. The owner of the space, an art collector himself, found the building's historic and architectural values a blank canvas for the design of his new home. The existing industrial features, such as exposed-brick walls and a rustic wood ceiling beam that runs the length of the loft, played a major role in the redesign.

Soho Loft

Eddie Lee

Manhattan, New York, United States

© Eric Piasecki

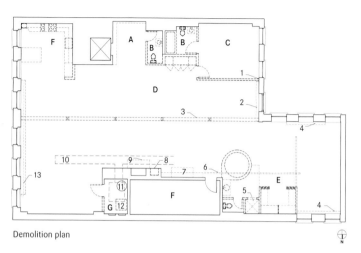

Demolition plan

A. Entry
B. Bathroom
C. Bedroom
D. Living area
E. Master suite
F. Fire staircase
G. Mechanical room

1. Remove any gypboard to expose brick beneath corner
2. Radiator 13-3/4" above finished floor to be removed
3. Existing beam above to remain

4. Radiator 14" above finished floor to be removed
5. Curb and shower pan to be removed and floor leveled
6. Existing main sprinkler feed to remain
7. Desk
8. Log box set in wall to be removed and filled in
9. Fireplace hearth to be removed
10. Existing HVAC above
11. Water heater
12. Existing washer and dryer
13. Radiator and bench to be removed

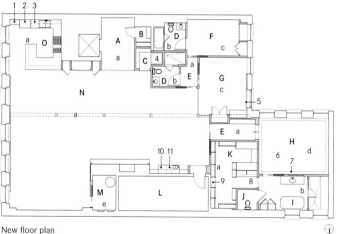

New floor plan

A. Entry
B. Coat closet
C. Utility room
D. Bathroom
E. Vestibule
F. Bedroom
G. Gym
H. Master bedroom
I. Master bathroom
J. Water closet
K. Dressing room
L. Fire staircase
M. Mechanical room
N. Living area
O. Kitchen

1. Pantry
2. Refrigerator
3. Dishwasher
4. Washer and dryer
5. Baseboard radiator
6. 12" raised platform with radiant floor heat
7. Wood border, one plank wide
8. Wood saddle, typical
9. Bench
10. Beverage center
11. Ice dispenser

a. Wood floor
b. Stone floor
c. Carpet
d. Carpet field
e. Painted floor

Creating a bright and open living space was one of the requirements. But with windows only at the front and back, opportunities to create a layout that would allow natural light to the middle of the loft were limited. This issue was resolved by enclosing a gym in glass so as not to block light through a rear window.

The central feature of the apartment is a
vibrant cobalt-blue fireplace wall, which
also proves an ideal foil for a Rashid
Johnson painting. Blue is also the main
accent color throughout, set against the
relaxing neutrals.

Custom pieces, such as an oversized
dining table modeled after one the
client had seen at a French château,
emphasize the rustic-industrial chicness
of the existing architectural elements.
Other, more contemporary items, such
as the dining chairs, counterbalance the
wood elements.

147

Simple color schemes are often the most powerful, effective way to create the desired atmosphere.

148

Bathrooms often receive the
least attention in terms of
design. However, beautiful
bathrooms can add quality
to our daily lives. Updating
key fixtures can transform a
bathroom into a relaxing, spa-
like retreat.

A young couple's urban residence is enriched with bursts of bold color and texture, transforming it into a modern and unique apartment full of strong and vibrant flavors. Modern pieces have been combined with playful accents and ethnic touches to create a space that is eclectic but undeniably urban, and is cool and relaxed, while still feeling grown-up. The use of simple graphic patterns and vivid colors tones down the existing woodwork and prevents the space from feeling overly rustic.

Loft Apartment

Fanny Abbes - The New Design Project

Jersey City, New Jersey, United States

© Alan Gastelum

Mood board

149

The use of simple graphic patterns and smooth, shiny surfaces can add some zest to a space dominated by woodsy elements and prevent it from feeling overly rustic.

Walnut buffet with brass accents from **Organic Modernism** topped by vintage black-and-white mushroom lamps from **Brooklyn Auction Barn**; copper pendants by Tom Dixon; and assorted Jean Prouvé Standard chairs around a walnut and white mid-century dining table from **Circa60** complete the setting of a warm and inviting dining area.

150

Artwork can be a key feature of interior décor. An art piece can complement the color scheme of a room, unify a design theme, or emphasize the character of an overall design composition.

A round jute rug as wall décor from **West Elm** and a cord bench from **CB2** add texture and harmonize with the ceiling rafters, while a **Beni Ourain**-inspired rug from **Burke Decor**, Shayk pendants from **Artecnica**, and a white-and-walnut dresser from **West Elm** bring in a retro flavor.

DIRECTORY

19 Greek Street
London, United Kingdom
www.19greekstreet.com

Art Buro
London, United Kingdom
www.artburo.co.uk

Beef Architekti
Bratislava, Slovakia
www.beef.sk

BUTZ + KLUG architecture
Boston, Massachusetts, United States
www.bkarch.com

Buratti Architetti
Milan, Italy
www.burattiarchitetti.it

Casa Botelho
London, United Kingdom
www.casabotelho.com

cityhomeCOLLECTIVE
Salt Lake City, Utah, United States
www.cityhomecollective.com

CM Natural Designs
San Diego, California, United States
www.cmnaturaldesigns.com

D'Aquino Monaco
New York, New York, United States
www.daquinomonaco.com

Dan Gayfer Design
Northcote, Victoria, Australia
www.dangayfer.com

Diego Revollo
São Paulo, Brazil
www.diegorevollo.com.br

Doherty Design Studio
Hawthorn, Victoria, Australia
www.dohertydesignstudio.com.au

Eddie Lee
New York, New York, United States
www.eddieleeinc.com

Eisner Design
New York, New York, United States
www.eisnerdesign.com

Escobar Design by Lemay
Montreal, Quebec, Canada
New York, New York, United States
www.escobardesign.com

Jenny Martin Design
Victoria, British Columbia, Canada
www.jennymartindesign.com

Jessica Gersten Interiors
New York, New York, United States
www.jessicagersteninteriors.com

Jo Berryman Studio
London, United Kingdom
www.joberryman.com

Jodie Cooper Design
Perth, Western Australia, Australia
www.jodiecooperdesign.com.au

Kelly and Co. Design
Redding, Connecticut, United States
www.kellyandcodesign.com

Les Ensembliers
Montreal, Quebec, Canada
Toronto, Ontario, Canada
www.ensembliers.com

LyonsKelly
Dublin, Ireland
www.lyonskelly.com

Menichetti+Caldarelli
Gubbio, Perugia, Italy
www.menichetti-caldarelli.it

New Design Project
Brooklyn, New York, United States
www.thenewdesignproject.com

Obllique
Singapore, Singapore
www.obllique.com

Ofist
Istanbul, Turkey
www.ofist.com

Pascali Semerdjian Arquitetos
São Paulo, Brazil
www.pascalisemerdjian.com

PROjECT
Chicago, Illinois, United States
www.projectinteriors.com

SAS \ Solomonoff Architecture Studio
New York, New York, United States
www.solomonoff.com

Shawn Henderson
New York, New York, United States
www.shawnhenderson.com

TANK Architecture & Interior Design
Amsterdam, The Netherlands
www.tank.nl

Techné Architects
Melbourne, Victoria, Australia
www.techne.com.au

Toledano + Architects
Tel Aviv, Israel
www.toledano-architects.com

Union Studio
Berkeley, California, United States
www.unionstudio.com

Waind Gohil Architects
London, United Kingdom
www.gpa.co.uk

ZWADA Home
Vancouver, British Columbia, Canada
www.zwadadesign.com